DUPLICATE BRIDGE

G.C.H. FOX

Duplicate Bridge

NEW YORK
St. Martin's Press

LONDON
Robert Hale & Company

© G.C.H. Fox 1974
First published in Great Britain 1974
First published in United States of America 1975

St. Martin's Press, Inc.
175 Fifth Avenue
New York, N.Y. 10010

Library of Congress Catalog Card Number 74-19856

Robert Hale & Company
63 Old Brompton Road
London, S.W. 7.

ISBN 0 7091 4803 8

Composed by Specialised Offset Services Ltd
and printed in Great Britain by Lowe & Brydone Ltd
Thetford, Norfolk.

CONTENTS

PREFACE

This book is primarily written for the large number of players who have never heard of duplicate bridge and do not, in fact, know that such a game exists.

Rubber bridge and duplicate are not totally different games with separate laws, although the rules necessarily differ in one or two particulars. But it is unknown to many that it is possible to play under conditions where it is immaterial whether you hold good or bad cards, since each one has the same chance in this respect.

It is also written for that ever increasing number who have tried duplicate, discovered its fascination and are now anxious to gain greater knowledge of the special tactical and strategical factors involved.

Part One is concerned mainly with a description of how duplicate bridge is played. It is not written for the Tournament Director and does not set out to describe intricate movements for pairs and teams contests. It merely describes the most common types of movement likely to be used in club tournaments, those that the ordinary player is likely to meet, and explains how such movements are carried out. With a good basic knowledge of these matters a player will not feel strange when he plays his first duplicate. He will be able to concentrate fully on his bidding and play without having to worry about what is going on around him. Furthermore, he will not be a liability to the Tournament Director, who will not have to spend much time and vigilance correcting inaccurate scores, frequent misboardings and so forth.

Indeed, if greater attention were paid to the duties incumbent on the players in any competition, the life of the Tournament Director would be a far happier one. Competitions would run more smoothly and quickly. Results would be known much earlier and the possibility of errors considerably reduced because of the greater care and accuracy displayed by players in entering the score. So, even if you are a regular and experienced duplicate player, you may very well profit by reading Part One.

Part Two is concerned purely with tactics. It must be appreciated that duplicate bridge is in some ways a different type of game from rubber bridge and that the employment of astute tactics and strategy may well have an important bearing on the result of the match or tournament.

Teams and Pairs competitions have been considered separately as the tactics required for each differ in many situations. I have also considered individually the technique required for competitions governed by aggregate scoring and those by match points.

Pairs tournaments are practically all now played with match point scoring.

Duplicate bridge in England is governed by the English Bridge Union (EBU) whose functions include organizing and running national competitions.

The English Bridge Union is made up of delegates from the various County Associations who organize their own programme of competitions for both experts and the less experienced players.

A player anxious to pay duplicate should contact his County Secretary, details of whom can be obtained from the EBU Secretary:

Mrs A. L. Fleming,
12 Frant Road,
Tunbridge Wells,
Kent.

Since *Duplicate Bridge* was first published some years ago many changes have been introduced. The original scale of IMPS has been altered and the sequence of dealer and vulnerability on the board have been changed to conform with other countries. In the new edition I have revised where necessary and added numerous hands from play, many from international matches and championships to illustrate the various aspects of duplicate.

G. C. H. FOX

PART ONE

PROCEDURE

1

THE MEANING OF DUPLICATE BRIDGE

The essential feature of duplicate bridge is that all competing players hold the same cards throughout the tournament and in that respect have an equal chance. The winner is not necessarily the player who holds the best cards, but the one who makes the best use of the material at his disposal.

It follows, therefore, that even if you sit throughout the session with bad hands and you are never able to make a bid, you can still win if you can do better than the other competitors who are holding the same poor cards as yourself.

To take a simple example. Suppose in a team of four match one pair bids and makes a vulnerable grand slam in spades, scoring 2210 points (the scoring will be explained later, see page 14). In the other room their opponents will hold the good cards and their team mates the poor ones. Now, if the other side bid only to a small slam, or alternatively fail to make their contract, there will be a large gain to one team. This gain will not be due to superior cards, for each had an equal opportunity.

Nearly all championships, tournaments and matches are played by the duplicate method. To do otherwise would evoke the obvious comment that one side won because they had all the cards. There have been important contests played under rubber bridge conditions. In 1932 Ely Culbertson challenged Sydney Lenz to a match of 150 rubbers to prove the superiority of his bidding system. Later, in 1935, a similar battle took place, again over 150 rubbers, between Mr & Mrs Culbertson and Mr & Mrs Hal Sims. More recently, in 1970, a challenge match of 100 rubbers was played in London between Jeremy Flint and Jonathon Cansino representing Crockfords Club and the Omar Sharif Bridge Circus comprising Omar Sharif, Benito Garozzo, Georgio Belladonna and Claude Delmouly.

These contests could only be regarded as a fair test because the number of rubbers played was sufficient to allow for the luck to even out. In fact, subsequent analysis showed that each side held very nearly the same number of aces and kings. As matches of his length are obviously impractical the solution is to play duplicate bridge.

Method of Play – Tricks

To ensure that all competitors have the same opportunity it is necessary that the hands remain intact so players must keep their cards in front of them and not throw them in the middle in the ·usual way. Winning cards are placed face downwards in front of the player, pointing to the centre of the table. Losing cards are placed horizontally so that at the end of the hand each player will have in front of him the original thirteen cards he was dealt. In the illustration below it can be seen that six tricks have been played, of which three have won and three have lost.

Boards

The thirteen cards are then returned to a receptacle called a board. This is a square or rectangular frame containing four pockets marked N, S, E and W representing the points of the compass. The player sitting in the North seat puts his thirteen cards back in the North slot, and the other players place their cards in their correct slot. In order that the cards should be replaced in their correct slots, many boards have an arrow pointing to North as it is considered that if the North player is right the remainder must also be correct.

In duplicate bridge each hand is a separate entity and rubbers are not scored. The scoring at duplicate is slightly different and will be described in the next section. One consequence of this is that the score is pre-ordained and is marked clearly on the board, as also is the dealer. The variations are:

> Neither side vulnerable (or Love All)
> North — South vulnerable
> East — West vulnerable
> Both sides vulnerable (or Game All)

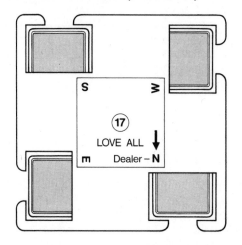

A popular form of "board" is the wallet type, which is lighter and less clumsy.

The vulnerability is indicated by a red band over the pocket of the relevant side. In the illustration below East — West are vulnerable

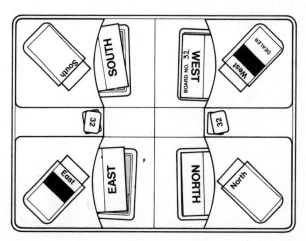

and West is marked as dealer. There is no arrow pointing to North.
There is an official sequence of vulnerability, as follows:

Board	1	Dealer	North	Love All
	2		East	North — South Vul.
	3		South	East — West Vul.
	4		West	Game All
	5		North	North — South Vul.
	6		East	East — West Vul.
	7		South	Game All
	8		West	Love All
	9		North	East — West Vul.
	10		East	Game All
	11		South	Love All
	12		West	North — South Vul.
	13		North	Game All
	14		East	Love All
	15		South	North — South Vul.
	16		East	East — West Vul.

A complete set of boards numbers 32 and boards 17-32 are identical
in dealer and vulnerability as boards 1-16.

Scoring

It has already been explained that in duplicate bridge each hand is a
separate entity of itself and the score on each hand is stated on the
board. As rubbers are not played a bonus is awarded for making games
and part scores, as follows:

Non-vulnerable game bid and made	Score 300
Vulnerable game bid and made	Score 500
Part score — whether vulnerable or not	Score 50

All other items of scoring such as penalties, slams etc. are normal
except that in most forms of duplicate there is no bonus for honours.

Example 1   Non Vulnerable
Contract Four Hearts. 10 tricks made. Score 420
    (120 trick score plus 300 for game)
Example 2   Vulnerable
Contract Six Spades. 12 tricks made. Score 1430
    (180 trick score plus 500 game and 750 little slam)

Example 3   Vulnerable or Non-Vulnerable

Contract Three Spades. 9 tricks made. Score 140

   (90 trick score plus 50 part score)

   Computing the score at duplicate is quite easy as you do not have to worry about the dividing line as in rubber bridge. Count all the tricks actually made and add the relevant bonus.

Example 4   Non Vulnerable

Contract four spades. 12 tricks made. Score 480

   (180 trick score plus 300 for game)

Example 5   Vulnerable or Non-Vulnerable

Contract two hearts. 10 tricks made. Score 170

   (120 for tricks plus 50 part score)

As game was not called you can only claim part score bonus.

Example 6   Non-Vulnerable

Contract One No Trump Doubled. 8 tricks made. Score 280.

   (Trick score = 80 (2 x 40) plus 100 for overtrick plus

   50 for contract and 50 for part score)

   The easy way to remember how to work out a doubled part score is to double the trick score and add 100. Thus two diamonds doubled = 180. (2 x 40 plus 100). But two spades doubled (vulnerable) = 670. (2 x 60 = 120 (game) Therefore add 500 apart from the bonus of 50 for contract.

   When scoring it is customary to put an asterisk to indicate double and two asterisks for redouble, e.g. 2S* (two spades doubled) 6H** (six hearts doubled and redoubled).

Misboarding

   The principle whereby players keep their cards in front of them, instead of grouping the cards into tricks as in rubber bridge, has been described earlier.

   The correct procedure is to place the cards in a clearly identifiable sequence. Some players place their winners one side and the losers the other. This is incorrect as it is not possible to reconstruct the play of a hand trick by trick to settle a dispute. Furthermore, if a player exercises his right to see the last trick there is a danger that the wrong card may be turned up.

   At the conclusion of the hand each player has a duty to check that he has put back the correct number of cards into the correct pocket of the board. It is the duty of all players to ensure that the board is placed correctly on the table so that the North player's cards are duly inserted in the North slot etc. It is a rule of duplicate bridge that the board must remain on the table during the bidding and play of each hand. This is to avoid the board being later misplaced. If cards are wrongly put back in any way this constitutes a "misboarding" and the offender may be penalised. In the same way, when a new board is placed on the table it is the duty of all players, after removing their cards from the slot, to count them face downwards before looking at them. If you find that you have fourteen and another player has only twelve, it is possible for the hand to be corrected provided that you have not seen it.

If you have looked at it and, after adjustment, you no longer hold the ace of hearts, for example, the hand cannot be played.

As a further safeguard it is customary, certainly in England, to use curtain or record cards. These are small coloured cards upon which the hand is recorded.

Board No. 7

NORTH

♠	K 5 3
♥	2
♦	K J 7 4
♣	K 10 7 5 2

The number of the hand corresponds to the number of the board. This should be written at the top in case the record card becomes mislaid and it can be identified. It is desirable that record cards should be of different colours to differentiate between the positions (North, South, etc.). If a player sees a "wrong" curtain card in his slot he can call the tournament director.

Having counted your cards face downwards it is wise to compare them with the record card. Do not, however, do what a certain experienced tournament player did. In order to impress the others he picked out his record card and bid from it without inspecting his cards. He received rather a shock when he found himself declarer in five diamonds with two small cards in the suit. The player who had written the card out had inadvertently put the clubs as diamonds and diamonds as clubs.

Comparison between Duplicate and Rubber Bridge

Duplicate bridge is not played for money. Stakes are expressly forbidden by the English Bridge Union in all competitions under their aegis. Sweepstakes are permitted, the winning players sharing the pool which is usually quite a modest sum. Therefore one important difference is that holding perpetually poor cards is not the same costly experience as in rubber bridge. There is nearly always something to play for in duplicate, particularly in contests where it matters greatly whether you make even ten more points than your rivals. To give a simple example. Suppose, playing rubber bridge the dealer opens a strong no trump and his partner raises to three no trumps, putting down 14 high card points. It is a near certainty that you will not defeat the contract and at rubber bridge it probably does not matter whether declarer makes 9, 10, 11 or even 12 tricks.

It is a dull hand for you as defender, possibly less so for the declarer. But at duplicate you may do just as well by holding the contract down to ten tricks in all as if you had bid and made a grand slam, for in your own way you may have obtained a superior result to any gained by those who held the same cards as yourself. This will be easier to understand when the scoring is explained in greater detail later (see page 37).

Duplicate bridge is the best way to improve the standard of your game. This is due to the fact that the same cards are played by others and it is possible to compare your results with theirs. For example, you are in four spades and go one down. In an ordinary game you might well contend that the contract was either most unlucky or that it was never to be made. You might even take the war into the enemy's camp and tell your partner he had no right to bid so high. Should he be rash enough to suggest you should have made it you tell him it was impossible. By this time the cards are all mixed together and no-one can prove anything. At duplicate, however, the records may show that four spades was bid and made at every other table and you were the only player to fail. It may now dawn upon you that you may not have played the hand to the best advantage. By discussing it with other players you can discover where you went wrong.

Or again, opponents bid up to three diamonds and you get them two down. You are probably well satisfied to have defeated them. If, however, you are looking at the travelling score sheet on which is recorded the previous results of the hand and discover that your side could have made four spades, you will realize that you have not made the best of your cards.

Another big difference lies in the tactics to be employed. This will be discussed fully in Part Two but one simple example may be cited here. Suppose that the opponents, vulnerable, bid up to four hearts. Playing rubber bridge and not wishing to let the rubber go without a fight, you bid five diamonds and are doubled and lose 500. All you can reasonably say at this stage is "Partner, let's hope it is worth it". Should the opponents bid and make game next hand you will have merely inflated the loss and it would have been cheaper to let them have the rubber. Not so at duplicate, where each hand is a separate entity and you know exactly what you can afford. If the opponents are stated to be vulnerable and bid up to four spades they will score 620 (120 plus 500).

If you are not vulnerable and bid five diamonds and lose 500, you have saved at least 120 points. You are not concerned with the next hand. If you miscalculate and go four down, losing 700, that is too much. This would be more serious in a pairs tournament than in teams as will be explained later in Part Two.

Luck in Duplicate

From the foregoing it might be thought that the element of chance is entirely excluded at duplicate and the result of any contest would depend solely on the skill of the respective contestants. This is not the case. It is impossible to eliminate the guesswork connected with a blind lead. It may also happen that a contract of three no trumps can be made from one side (e.g. North) and not by the other. There may be no fault to find in the bidding and it may be completely fortuitous whether North or South is declarer.

In pairs contests luck plays a big part. You may, on a particular hand, be opposed by a strong pair who bid a slam which others have not reached, or make a difficult contract requiring skill not possessed by other competitors. Nor is it any credit to you if your opponents, by bad bidding, reach a contract in no trumps which has no chance, when all the others holding their cards reach four hearts which cannot be defeated.

Important matches are usually long, 64 or possibly 100 hands. This allows for luck to even out. Important pairs championships are also played to extend over at least three sessions and there is a good possibility that the best pairs will finish near the top. But ordinary tournaments in clubs cannot last longer than the time allowed for one evening's play and consequently the luck element must exist. This is not a bad thing for it enables weaker players to have their periodic success.

The main point to stress is that the luck of the cards is eliminated and in that respect all competitors have the same chance so far as good and bad cards are concerned.

2

CONTESTS BETWEEN TEAMS

Two Teams of Four
The simplest form of match is between two teams of four. Suppose the two teams are made up of:

Team 1   Mr & Mrs A and Mr & Mrs B
Team 2   Mr & Mrs X and Mr & Mrs Y

The usual procedure is for each table to be in a separate room so that one does not overhear what is happening at the other. Let us suppose that in one room Mr & Mrs A are sitting North – South against Mr & Mrs X. In the other room Mr & Mrs Y will be occupying the North – South seats against Mr & Mrs B.

	Room One			*Room Two*	
	Mr A			Mr Y	
	North			North	
Mrs X		MrX	Mrs B		Mr B
West		East	West		East
	Mrs A			Mrs Y	
	South			South	

If the match is a normal short match of 32 boards (or hands), the players will seat themselves as in the diagram in Room one and will take boards 1-8 with Room two taking boards numbered 9-16. At the commencement each hand must be dealt to bring it into being. In each room eight hands are dealt and played, the cards being kept apart and replaced accurately in the correct pocket of the board. If it should happen that a hand is passed out, no player making a bid, the hand counts as played, there being no score to either side. Merely because no-one bids in one room is no guarantee that there will be no bidding in the other. It is quite possible for a game to be bid and made.

When boards 1-8 have been dealt and played in Room one and boards 9-16 in Room two, these are exchanged so that Room one will play boards 9-16 and Room two boards 1-8. The cards must not be redealt as they have already been played. In fact, at the end of the first half all sixteen boards will have been played by both teams.

Furthermore, owing to the seating of the players, each side will have had the same opportunity of playing the same cards.

At the end of 16 boards it is half time and the normal practice is for the teams to foregather and compare scores. The method of recording scores on each hand will be described later (see page 23).

After comparing scores the teams re-seat themselves but with different opponents. Thus:

	Room One			*Room Two*	
	Mr A			Mr X	
	North			North	
Mrs Y		Mr Y	Mrs B		Mr B
West		East	West		East
	Mrs A			Mrs X	
	South			South	

The procedure is similar to the first half. Room one will take boards 17-24 and Room two boards 25-32. Each will deal and play the hands as before since these eight boards have not yet been played. The boards are again inter-changed until both rooms have played a further sixteen hands, making thirty-two in all. The final score is then agreed and the result of the match decided.

It is not essential to use a set of 32 boards. If only 16 are available they can be reshuffled and replayed. Nor is it essential to play 32 hands. If time is short it is quite in order to play 24. In this case the match may be divided into two halves of 12, one room starting with boards 1-6 and the other 7-12. When these have all been played and the half time score agreed, the second half will be played, using boards 13-24.

In matches, teams usually consist of four, five or six players, the remaining two being reserves. In most cases the rules provide that reserves can be introduced at the break, i.e. after 16 boards. It is also quite usual to divide a match of 32 boards into four sessions of eight boards each, comparing scores after 8, 16, 24 and 32. This enables changes in line up to be made after playing 8 boards.

The order of seating teams is decided by tossing. The losers must place their team and their opponents then place their pairs as they consider best. The right to be the last to seat one's team passes alternately. The reason is chiefly one of tactics, choosing the pair most likely to do well against certain opponents.

In Cup competitions and later rounds of important competitions matches may consist of 48, 64 or even 100 boards and on these occasions play will extend over two or three sessions.

In some competitions the rules stipulate that the captain must play an equal number of boards with each member of his team. Where this rule applies the match is divided into three equal parts, a normal short match being 30 boards divided into three sets of 10 boards. Whatever the length of a match it is most improper for one team, should it finish first, to enter the other room so as to watch the remaining hands being played. Apart from the fact that it is apt to put the players off, there is an ever present temptation to let drop injudicious remarks, such as a whispered aside "This is the hand where we should have bid a slam", or some such comment.

When matches are played in clubs it is not uncommon for one or two club members to watch. This is in order, providing they first ask permission. But onlookers (or kibitzers as they are termed) should not "follow the boards"; that is to say, having watched the boards being played in one room they must not go to the other room and watch them being played a second time.

Scoring

There are two principle methods of scoring:

(a) *Aggregate*

(b) *International Match Points* (IMPS)

In each case players should record the contract and the points won or lost on the personal score card provided for this purpose.

These are fairly self-explanatory. The number on the left corresponds to the number of the hand and many cards also give the dealer and vulnerability. It is merely a question of entering up the contract, the declarer, and points won or points lost. The column headed "Versus pair number" is not used in straight matches between two teams. It is necessary in multiple team contests and pairs events and this will be explained later (see pages 27 and 31).

Deal Hand No. Vul.		Versus Team or Pair No.	Final Contract	By	Tricks	SCORE		MATCH POINTS	
						PLUS	MINUS		
N	1–								
E	2NS								
S	3EW								
W	4ALL								
N	5NS								
E	6EW								
S	7ALL	3	45	N	10	620		12	
W	8–	3	3H	E	9		140		6
N	9EW	3	3NT	E	8	100		12	
E	10ALL								
S	11–								
W	12NS								
N	13ALL								
E	14–								
S	15NS								
W	16EW								
					Totals				

Scale of International Match Points

0 – 10	0	270 – 310	7	900 – 1090	14	2500 – 2740	21
20 – 40	1	320 – 360	8	1100 – 1290	15	2750 – 2990	22
50 – 80	2	370 – 420	9	1300 – 1490	16	3000 – 3240	23
90 – 120	3	430 – 490	10	1500 – 1740	17	3250 – 3490	24
130 – 160	4	500 – 590	11	1750 – 1990	18	3500 and up	25
170 – 210	5	600 – 740	12	2000 – 2240	19		
220 – 260	6	750 – 890	13	2250 – 2490	20		

(a) *Aggregate*. This is the easiest method and merely consists of totalling up the points that you have won, subtracting the points you have lost and ascertaining the difference. The points are scored in accordance with the normal duplicate rules given on page 14. The usual bonus for honours is counted.

Suppose that in our first example the results are as follows:

First half. Boards 1-16 Mr & Mrs A + 3210 in Room One

          Mr & Mrs Y + 1820 in Room Two

At half time Mr A's team lead by 1390 points.

Suppose that in the second half, boards 17-32

Mr & Mrs A + 1000 in Room One

Mr & Mrs X + 2500 in Room Two

Mr Y's team has recovered 1500 points and wins by 110.

Aggregate scoring is not used so frequently now. The chief criticism of this method is that one big swing caused by a freak deal may well decide a match. For example, suppose one team bids seven spades vulnerable and the opening lead is trumped. The team loses 100 for going one down undoubled. Their opponents play in seven hearts and make it. This will give them a score of 2210 (210 for tricks, 500 for game and 1500 for grand slam). The total gain of 2310 may be impossible to recover in the space of 32 hands and the match is virtually won or lost on one hand.

(b) *International Match Points* (IMPS). By this method each team compares the results board by board, converting the gains and losses into match points in accordance with the graded scale as follows:

Scale of International Match Points

Difference on Board	IMPS
0 — 10	0
20 — 40	1
50 — 80	2
90 — 120	3
130 — 160	4
170 — 210	5
220 — 260	6
270 — 310	7
320 — 360	8
370 — 420	9
430 — 490	10
500 — 590	11
600 — 740	12
750 — 890	13
900 — 1090	14
1100 — 1290	15
1300 — 1490	16
1500 — 1740	17
1750 — 1990	18
2000 — 2240	19

2250 – 2490	20
2500 – 2740	21
2750 – 2990	22
3000 – 3240	23
3250 – 3490	24
3500 or over	25

Example 1. Love All

Team A bids four spades – making 10 tricks = 420 (120 + 300)
Team B bids three spades – making 10 tricks = 170 (120 + 50)
Team A gain 250 points = 6 IMPS

Example 2. North – South Vulnerable

Team A, playing East – West are three down doubled in five clubs – lose 500

Team B, playing East – West in the other room, let their opponents play in four spades, which is made to score 620 (120 + 500)

Team A therefore gain 120 points = 3 IMPS

Example 3. Game All

Team A bid and make two spades = 110 (60 + 50)

Team A with the opposite cards, bid and make three diamonds = 110 (60 + 50)

Team A have scored in both rooms and gain 220 points = 6 IMPS

Example 4. Game All

Team A bid four spades and make 12 tricks = 680

Team B bid six spades and make 12 tricks = 1430

Team B gain 750 points = 13 IMPS

Under this method honours are not counted. The object of the scale is to control the amount won or lost on one hand.

In the example given on page 55, where an aggregate gain of 2410 occurred on a freak hand, this would represent 20 IMPS. This amount could be recovered in two hands where game was made in one room and defeated in the other.

Multiple Teams Contests

It is possible for three or more teams to compete against each other at the same time. The procedure is not as simple as with two teams, but is not unduly complicated. The movement is easiest when an odd number of teams is competing.

American Whist League Movement

This is the method commonly used in congress and club events.

At the commencement players sit at a table as a team. That is to say all the members of the team are seated at the same table. The tables are numbered consecutively and each team is designated by the number of the table it occupies at the start. The boards are then distributed in rotation commencing at table one, the same number being placed on each table. This will depend on the number of boards to be played, which will in turn depend on the number of tables. For example, if there are eleven tables (11 teams) you can put out either 22 or 33 boards. Since no team plays against itself, either 20 or 30 boards will be played. The number of boards will depend largely on the time available for the contest.

Each team decides which pair will sit North – South and which East – West. At the first move the East – West pair in each team move down two tables, the boards remaining on the original table. For example, the East – West pair at table seven would move to table five. If there are nine tables, the East – West pair at table one would move to table eight. On the first round the cards in the boards must be shuffled and dealt. When the hand has been played the cards are returned accurately into the correct slot. At each table players must keep their score carefully on the private score card and here the column relating to the opposing team's number must be filled in. If, for example, you are playing boards 7-9 at table three you must put 3 in the column on the left (see illustration on page 24).

East – West pairs will find that they play their boards in strict numerical order. Thus after playing boards 9 and 10, they will play boards 7 and 8 etc. Their opponents' numbers will also go down in twos (7 5 3 1, etc). North – South will play their boards in strict numerical order. If a set of boards arrives out of sequence the tournament director should be called since something has gone wrong and should be corrected at once.

When the first set of boards has been played the East – West pairs move down two tables and leave the boards one table down, e.g. from table seven East – West move to table five, leaving the boards they have played on table six. They will continue to move in this way until final round which would bring them back to their own table and the other half of their team.

They will then compare their scores and convert these into IMPS in accordance with the scale given on pages 24-26.

It is important that in a multiple teams contest you enter the number of the opposing team in the column provided as this information will be required by the tournament director to check the scores. It is usual for one North – South and one East – West card to be handed to the tournament director after play so that scores can be checked. Therefore each player in the team should keep his score. It is also wise to check the scores with opponents before leaving the table. This all assists in getting a quick and accurate result.

By altering the initial move it is possible to arrange for some matches to be concluded half way through the session so that scores can then be worked out. The practice is common in congress events where it is convenient to have a break for teas or refreshments and teams can join up and work out a half-time score.

Victory Points

In some tournaments international match points may be converted into victory points, according to a fixed scale. If, for example, each team were to play 6 boards with each opponent, the net difference in IMPS would be worked out and then converted to victory points. The following is an example of the scale:

Difference in IMPS on 6 Boards	Victory Points
0 – 1	6 – 6
2 – 4	7 – 5
5 – 9	8 – 4
10 – 14	9 – 3
15 – 20	10 – 2
21 – 27	11 – 1
27 or over	12 – 0

Victory points are also used in straight matches between two teams particularly in major events, such as the European Championships. As matches are of 32 boards the scale is larger and there are twenty victory points at stake. If one team wins by an exceptionally large margin they receive 20 victory points and their opponents may be debited with up to minus 3 victory points.

Convention Card

Before leaving this chapter, some mention should be made of the data to be entered on the front of the score card. This applies to both teams and pairs competitions. The illustration below is a simple example, giving the basis system, range of no trumps, slam conventions and other matters which need to be decided by partners and which have to be made known to the opponents.

MAYFAIR BRIDGE STUDIO
Telephone : 01-499 2844

Name J. BROWN   No. 5

Partner's Name MRS F. SMITH   Score

BIDS and CONVENTIONS

Basic System ACOL

Opening 1 N.T. ......Non Vul 12-14 ....Vul 15-17 .....4th hand. 12-14
(give point count)

Opening 2 bids ACOL

Opening 3 bids WEAK

1 N.T. overcall STRONG

Jump overcalls INTERMEDIATE

Defence of 1 N.T. SHARPLES

Defence to Pre-Empts LOWER MINOR

Slam conventions BLACKWOOD. GERBER

Leads A from AKx Signals NORMAL

Discards NORMAL

Other conventions FLINT, UNUSUAL NT
TRANSFER BIDS OVER INT.
STAYMAN · MICHAELS CUE BIDS·

3

PAIRS CONTESTS

MITCHELL MOVEMENT

This is the most common form of competition between pairs. The number of tables does not greatly matter but should not be less than five nor greater than fifteen.

The players are seated as pairs at tables which are numbered consecutively from one upwards. Half the contestants sit North – South and the other half East – West. It is usual to make one end of the room North so that each North player is occupying the same relative position. Whether players sit North – South or East – West can be left to chance (e.g. by tossing or drawing cards) or it can be pre-arranged. It might, for example, be desirable to divide up the strongest pairs so that they should not all be seated on the same side.

Players take their number from the table at which they are seated at the commencement of the tournament. Thus the pair sitting North – South at table three are North – South Pair 3 and their opponents East – West Pair 3, and they retain these numbers for the entire session. If there are a great number of tables, as often is the case at a bridge congress, it is usual to divide them up into sections. Thus a pair might be North-South Pair 3 in Section 1 or the Blue Section. Before play starts each pair should write their name clearly and legibly, together with their pair number, and section (if any) on the sheet of paper provided for the purpose. This information will be needed by the Tournament Director for entering in the results chart.

SECTION No. 1
N.S. PAIR No. 3 *J. Smith and H. Brown*
E.W. PAIR No. 3 *Mr. and Mrs. Robinson*

The boards are then distributed to the tables, an equal number on each depending on how many tables are in play. The normal number of boards played in a session will average between 24 and 30. Thus, if there are nine tables, 3 will be placed on each table — 27 boards in all, e.g.

Table One	Table Four	Table Seven
Boards 1-3	Boards 10-12	Boards 19-21
Table Two	Table Five	Table Eight
Boards 4-6	Boards 13-15	Boards 22-24
Table Three	Table Six	Table Nine
Boards 7-9	Boards 16-18	Boards 25-27

It is easy to check that the correct boards have been placed on the right table by multiplying the number of the table by the number of boards on the table. The result should be the number of the highest numbered board of the set, e.g.

Table Five	$3 \times 5 = 15$	Boards should be $13 - 14 - 15$.
Table Eight	$3 \times 8 = 24$	Boards should be $22 - 23 - 24$.

For the first round the cards must be shuffled and dealt to create a hand. The hand is then bid and played in the normal way, the cards, of course, being placed in front of each player and not pitched into the middle. If all players pass the hand is "thrown in" but it must not be re-dealt. At the end of the hand each player must write his hand on the hand record card (see page 16) and place it in the correct pocket of the board with the record card at the top and visible, but naturally turned face downwards so that the writing cannot be seen. The North player must then enter the details of the contract and score on the travelling score sheet. This will be described later under "Scoring" (pages 37-39).

When each table has completed their three boards the first move will be made. The East — West players all move to the next higher numbered table and the boards will be passed to the next lower numbered table. It is the duty of the North — South pair to pass the boards down. On the second round the boards will in most cases have already been dealt and played, so that each player merely has to take the correct hand out, count the cards face downwards and check with the record card. Eventually the East — West pair will have played at each table and all the boards will have been played. The tournament is ended and the Tournament Director will work out the scores and the result.

If the number of tables is even it is necessary to have what is termed a relay. This is the equivalent of a spare table placed exactly at the half-way stage. For example, if there are eight tables the relay would be placed between tables four and five and on it would be placed boards 13-15. On table five would be 16-18 and on six boards 19-21. Boards 22-24 would be on table seven, leaving none for table eight; table eight would share boards 1-3 with table one and would continue to share throughout the tournament. It may be more convenient for table one to share with table two, and in this case the relay table will be one further up, i.e. between five and six. Put another way, disregarding the two sharing tables, there must be an equal number of tables each side of the relay, e.g. Tables three, four, five Relay 6 7 8.

The relay is actually a table at which no-one is sitting. The boards from the table numbered immediately above it are passed on to the relay and the boards on the relay table are passed to the table numbered immediately below. A relay table is necessary to avoid the same players meeting the same boards twice in a session.

An alternative method of coping with an even number of tables is to employ a skip. The boards are laid out normally with no relay and the movement is normal for the first half of the tournament. At the half-way stage the East — West pairs move up two tables, the boards being passed one table down as usual. If this did not happen the East — West pairs would be due to play boards they had had before. On the last round the East — West pair will return to their original table and play a further two hands against their original opponents, unless it is decided to omit the last round due to the time factor. This method has the obvious disadvantage that each pair does not play every other pair but may play against one pair twice. But it is convenient when the number of tables is high, say 10 and 12. With a relay and 12 tables, two tables are sharing two boards and if one is slow the whole movement is held up. With 10 tables it might not be convenient to play 30 boards and 20 is too few. With a skip, omitting the last round, you play 27, a suitable number for the average session.

In a Mitchell movement the North — South pairs will always receive their boards in strict numerical order. Looking back at the diagram on page 32 it will be seen that on the second round the boards from table two, (four, five, six) will be passed down to table one which will have started with 1 2 3. The East — West pairs will play their boards in alternate sets. Thus East — West at table one, starting with boards 1-3 will move up to table two and play boards 7-9, originally at table three.

A Mitchell movement will normally provide two winners, one North — South and one East — West. Where it is desirable to have one winner only, as in the case of a competition final, the Howell movement is used. (see below).

Incomplete Table.

If there is one pair over they constitute a 'half table' and it is customary for them to sit East — West. For the round when they have no opponents they sit out. After the round they move to the next higher numbered table in the normal way. In the course of one session each East — West pair will sit out for one set of boards and will receive either an average score or no score at all, depending on the local rule. It is immaterial as it is the same for all East — West pairs.

HOWELL MOVEMENT

This type of movement is employed when the number of tables is small, between three and eight. It provides that each pair plays against every other pair and produces one eventual winner.

Players seat themselves at tables as a pair and derive their number from the guide card on the table.

Thus, if the guide card states that on round one the North — South is 3 and the East — West pair is 6, the pair occupying these positions will take these numbers. They will not be North — South 3 or East — West 6 but simply pair 3 or pair 6, for unlike a Mitchell movement pairs will sometimes play North — South and sometimes East — West. The only exception is that a pair, or pairs, will remain stationary throughout. An equal number of boards is played at each table depending on numbers. With seven tables, involving 14 pairs, two boards would be played each round with a total of 26 boards. This means that each pair plays two boards against each of the other competing partnerships.

Players move at the end of each round in accordance with the instructions on the guide card. The simplest way is to take notice of the pair you follow, particularly if easily spotted. It is easier, for example, to look for a large woman with a bright red hat than to keep looking at the guide card every time you move.

TABLE 1   REMAIN STATIONARY   TABLE 1

SOUTH

Howell Movement
for
6 PAIRS

ORIGINAL BOARDS
1-4

**CHECK YOUR BOARD NUMBERS
AND POSITION EVERY ROUND**

GO NEXT TO TABLE 3 E-W   **EAST**   **WEST**   GO NEXT TO TABLE 3 E-W

PAIRS TAKE NUMBERS INDICATED
IN FIRST ROUND

Rd.	N–S	E–W	BOARDS	
1.	6	1	1–4 or 1–5	
2.	6	2	5–8	6–10
3.	6	3	9–12	11–12
4.	6	4	13–16	16–20
5.	6	5	17–20	21–25

NORTH
REMAIN STATIONARY

TABLE 1   TABLE 1

SCRAMBLED MITCHELL (ARROW SWITCH)

If it is desired to have one winner and it is convenient to play a Mitchell movement, this can be achieved by using an arrow switch. That is to say for one or two rounds the East – West pairs play as North – South and vice versa. With a scrambled movement it is necessary for the East – West pairs to add a number to their designation, e.g. with seven tables the East – West pairs would add 7 to their table number, so that East – West pair 1 would become pair 8. Care is needed in entering the score when the arrow switch is in operation.

As stated above, in Howell movements there is always one stationary pair, usually the highest number. At each table the boards are played in strict consecutive order. But this does not mean that the pairs play the boards in consecutive order; only the stationary pair will do this.

In all Pairs contests it is important to remember the following rules, which apply to all forms of duplicate bridge.

(1) Be careful to count your cards face downwards as soon as you take them out of the board, and also when putting them back.

(2) If hand record cards are used be careful to replace the record card on top of the cards. This enables a player to recognize an irregularity if the wrong card (e.g. East) is in the West pocket.

(3) Be careful to ensure that the cards are restored to the correct pocket. The present rule is that the board should remain on the table during the bidding and play and this will ensure, to some extent, that the North pocket will remain facing the North player.

It is courteous, but not strictly obligatory, to sort your hand before putting it back in the board. Apart from the fact that it saves both time and trouble for the next player, there is a further reason. Suppose that the first two hands of a set you play are jumbled up and the third is sorted, there is a reasonable inference that the third hand was thrown in at the previous table.

SCORING

(a) *Aggregate*

Each pair merely adds up all the points won and lost. The balance, after subtraction represents their score. The winning total may be either plus or minus depending whether the players have had good or bad cards. If, for example, North – South have held overwhelming cards and their winning pair are plus 9500, it might be that the winning East – West score might be minus 1740. If all the East – West pairs held very bad cards, clearly the winners would be the pair who lost the least. In order to control, to some extent, over-large swings it is customary to limit the size of penalties, according to vulnerability. Thus, if an East – West pair go down 2000 their North – South opponents can only score 800, the balance being regarded as excess penalty. The losers, of course, debit their entire loss.

The purpose of this is to prevent one pair from winning the tournament owing to one colossal penalty. The usual scale for limitation of penalties is this:

When winners are vulnerable	800
When winners are not vulnerable	600

The recipients of a penalty are entitled to more when they are vulnerable as they were in a position to score more. There is no limitation if the final contract is a slam, either grand or small.

Honours are scored independently of the penalty so it would be possible to gain 900 if the penalty amounted to 800 or more and you held four honours in one hand.

Aggregate scoring is rarely used and the popular method of scoring pairs contests is by:

(b) *Match Points*

The principle is that a pair gains 2 match points from each pair, sitting in the same direction, for that particular hand, whose result is inferior to their own. It does not matter whether the margin is 10 points or 1000, the best score on each board is called a 'top'. The worst score is called a 'bottom'. Midway between the two is average. If there are 6 pairs competing against you (which will happen in the case of a seven table movement) and you obtain a better score than all the other pairs in your line, you will get a top which will be 12 match points. As you will receive 2 match points for each pair you beat and there are six pairs, you will win 12 match points (6 x 2). In other words the top is always the number of tables, less one, multiplied by two. For those who are algebraically minded, assuming the number of tables to be x, the top is $2 (x - 1)$. If there is a half-table the simplest method is to omit the pair sitting out and calculate according to the number of complete tables, e.g. 6½ tables count as 6 tables — top = 10.

Travelling Score Slip

Attached to each board is a travelling score slip, bearing the number of the board and, if there are more than one, the number or designation of the section. The sheet is more or less a recorded history of all the results that occur on that particular hand.

On the left are numbers ranging from one upwards and this number refers to the North — South pair. In the next column is placed the number of the East — West pair. The next columns are for entering the final contract, the declarer (i.e. N S E or W) and the result from the point of view of North — South. These are headed:

N — S Plus   N — S Minus

The remaining spaces are for entering up the match points and do not concern the players. They are the responsibility of the Tournament Director. At the conclusion of the hand the North player opens the slip and records the result of the hand just played. He records the information on the line opposite the number that represents his pair number. Thus, if he is Pair 1 he will always enter the score on the top line. The number on the left always refers to the North — South pairs; they do *not* refer to the number of the board. If the North — South pair have shown a loss on the hand the score will be put in the right hand column headed N – S Minus. If extra tricks are gained it is usual to put + after the contract.

Similarly, if the contract is defeated it is usual to put – e.g.:

4 S + 1 means 4 spades bid and 11 tricks made

3 H - 1 means 3 hearts bid and only 8 tricks made.

A doubled contract is usually indicated by an asterisk and a redoubled contract by two asterisks, e.g.:

4 S* = 4 spades doubled.

3 NT** = 3 NT doubled and redoubled.

Honours are not counted in match pointed pairs contests nor is there any limitation of penalties.

On no account whatever must the travelling score sheet be looked at before the hand has been completed. It is also most improper for dummy to look at the travelling sheet during the play of the hand.

Opposite is an illustration of a travelling score sheet completed. It is assumed to relate to Board 2 where North – South are vulnerable.

The scores are explained as follows:

N.S. 1   Bid and made 4 spades and are above average as there are only two better scores their way.

N.S. 2   Played the hand in No Trumps and also made 10 tricks.
As they score an extra 10 points (No Trumps) their score is slightly better than N.S. 1 and they are second top.

N.S.3   Also played in No Trumps but made only 9 tricks. Their score of 600 is inferior to Pair 1 who scored 620 and they get just average, for there are three better scores and three worse.

N.S. 4   Score a top. Their East – West opponents sacrificed in clubs and went four down doubled, costing 700. This was a bigger score than any other North – South pair. East – West knew they could not make five clubs but they hoped to be only three down (500) which would have been less than the value of a vulnerable game (600). Owing to poor play and probably good defence they were one more down than they hoped. See below, Pair 6.

N.S. 5   Here East – West probably called five clubs but North – South considered that the penalty might be only 500 and that a contract of five spades was safe. Unfortunately the contract went one down and N.S. 5 scored a bottom as theirs was the only minus score.

N.S. 6 Here East — West were only three down in five clubs and North — South gained only 500, less than most of the pairs in their line. The East — West pair therefore scored above average as their loss was smaller than four others in their line, who had all lost at least 600.

N.S. 7   Passed the hand out. Presumably North — South failed to open the bidding and missed a game. They do not quite score a bottom as they did not lose points (see N.S. 5). But they did not gain any and their score (zero) is next to bottom.

BOARD No. 2.

NORTH Player enters N.S + / — score only

* **Do not write in last two columns**   • •

N.S. Pair No.	E.W. Pair No.	CONTRACT	BY	NORTH-SOUTH Plus	NORTH-SOUTH Minus	N.S. Match Points	E.W. Match Points
1	1	4S	N	620		8	4
2	3	3NT+1	S	630		10	2
3	5	3NT	S	600		6	6
4	7	5C*−4	W	700		12	0
5	2	5S−1	N		100	0	12
6	4	5C*−3	W	500		4	8
7	6	Thrown in.				2	10
8							
9							
10							
11							
12							
13							
14							
15							
16							

4

INDIVIDUAL AND PAR CONTESTS

INDIVIDUAL CONTESTS are tournaments where each competitor plays with each other and there is one winner. The commonest numbers are 25, 20, 16 and 8 players.

It is usual for the boards to be played in groups of five so that the scores can be announced at regular intervals. This may influence the tactics of players who are doing very well or very badly.

The players are numbered 1-20, or according to the entry, and each is provided with a card stating where he is to go each round.

Individual tournaments are not over popular. They are slow and it is considered that the element of luck is high. Players constantly complain that they have been "fixed" by unskilled partners.

PAR CONTESTS are designed as a test of bidding and play technique, the element of luck being eliminated as far as possible.

A certain number of hands are prepared by the "hand setter" and each of these contains some point of bidding, play or defence. Marks are awarded for each hand, the pair or player scoring the most wins. The usual procedure is as follows. Players can sit anywhere but should retain their geographical positions (N/S and E/W) throughout. The board is placed on the table and the hand is bid in the normal way. At the end of the auction a paper marked "Bidding Slip" is opened. This gives a directed final contract and suggested bidding. If the players have reached this contract, no matter by what means, they score the points awarded. Their opponents may also score points for bidding to a certain level or passing. For example if the directed contract were six spades by South and West held the aces of clubs and diamonds he would probably gain points for not doubling since the double of a freely bid slam on two aces is unsound.

Whatever contract may have been reached, the hand is played in the Directed Contract, e.g. four hearts by South. The West player then selects his opening lead and places it face downwards on the table, while the "Lead Slip" is opened.

If he is correct he scores a point and faces his card. If not, he substitutes the recommended card.

Thereafter the hand is played out. At the end the "Play Slip" is read and this states whether the contract should be made or defeated and what points are given to the declarer or defenders.

In order to prevent a contract being made by a fluke or through poor defence it may be necessary to give players certain directions. For example, East defending against Four Hearts might be instructed "To return a trump when in with the ace" or "Do not discard a club".

It may also be desirable to state that the points can only be won if the hand has been played in a certain way. Here is an example of a Par hand.

South Dealer
Love All

```
                        North
                        ♠ 5 4 3
                        ♡ 7 6 5 4 2
                        ◇ 7 6
                        ♣ 9 8 5
West                                        East
♠ -                                         ♠ Q J 9 7
♡ J 3                                       ♡ 10 9 8
◇ Q J 10 9 8 5 3 2                          ◇ A K
♣ J 3 2                                     ♣ Q 10 6 4
                        South
                        ♠ A K 10 8 6 2
                        ♡ A K Q
                        ◇ 4
                        ♣ A K 7
```

Bidding Awards

N.S. for bidding four spades or four hearts or doubling five diamonds if bid   3 points

E.W. for bidding diamonds but not beyond the limit of five 2 points.

Suggested Bidding:

S	W	N	E
2 C	4 D	-	-
4 S	-	-	-

Directed Contract   four spades to be played by South.

Lead   ◊ Q   1 point.

Directions to East   East to lead a diamond at trick two.

Play Awards   N.S. for taking ten tricks *but only* if South ruffed second diamond with ♠6   5 points.

N.S. for ruffing with ♠6 but failing to make ten tricks   2 points.

Note on Play

South ruffs diamond return with ♠6 and lays down ♠Ace, discovering bad break.

South cashes top hearts and clubs, existing with third club.

If East wins and plays a club, South ruffs with ♠2 and over-ruffs in dummy with ♠4 to play through East.

If West wins and leads a diamond, North ruffs and South either over-ruffs, or under-ruffs with ♠2, depending whether East trumps or discards a club.

Par Contests are interesting and instructive, but their success depends upon the hands set. Some recent contests have shown a tendency to make the hands unduly freakish and abstruse. A few bizarre hands add colour and excitement but it is best to cater for the known ability of the competitor. It is demoralizing to score zero on every hand and a well produced competition should provide a fair test of good technique.

Par Contests require a lot of preparation and for this reason they seem to be a rare event.

PART TWO

TACTICS

5

TEAMS OF FOUR/AGGREGATE SCORING

BIDDING

(a) *Part Score*

The obvious, but nevertheless important, principle regarding contests governed by aggregate, is that you aim to build up the largest possible plus and the smallest possible minus. Every point counts. At the same time, although it is not practical to risk a heavy loss in order to achieve a small gain, it can be costly to play ultra safe and bid only when game is likely.

The early successes of the Acol team led by the late Harrison Gray about 1936 were to a large extent attributable to the importance attached by the team to contesting part scores and securing the contract in both rooms. It is surprising how part scores mount up. If one half of the team plays in two spades and scores 110 (60 + 50) and the other half, holding the opposite cards, bids and makes three diamonds (110) the total gain is 220. If this occurs five times in a match over 1000 points have been gained.

The safest way to buy the contract cheaply is to strike the first blow and open the bidding whenever possible. The bid must, of course, conform to the normal standards so far as playing strength and defensive tricks are concerned, but if the hand is at all reasonable it is very much better to open than wait and come in later. Holding, for example:

> ♠   K J 9 8 6 4
> ♡   7 5
> ◇   A Q 7
> ♣   5 4

open one spade. If the next player cannot risk a bid at the two level and partner supports your suit, you have already gone a long way towards silencing the fourth player who may have the best hand at the table. If the spades are not supported they are long enough to rebid. Failure to open might well result in your side being frozen out. Alternatively you might decide to enter the bidding in a later round and at a higher level and get doubled and lose 500.

(b) Games

Other factors being equal it is correct to bid a non-vulnerable game, provided its success depends upon as good as an even money chance, such as a finesse. The difference between missing and making a non-vulnerable game is not great and therefore inferior odds should not be accepted. For example, suppose you play in three spades, making ten tricks and your opponents bid and make game:

you score	90 + 30 + 50	= 170
they score	120 + 300	= 420

Your net loss = 250

Suppose you bid game and go down one trick and your opponents play in a part score making nine tricks:

you lose	50
they score	140

Your net loss = 190

Assuming that the decision is relatively close and you are unlikely to be doubled, the loss by under-bidding is only 60.

The loss of a vulnerable game is more serious. Let us suppose in the previous example your side is vulnerable:

Stopping in three spades and making ten tricks	score 170
Opponents bid and make four spades	score 620

Net loss = 450

Bidding game and going one down	- 100
Opponents bid and make three spades	+ 140

Net loss = 240

So that, assuming a double and heavy defeat is unlikely, you stand to lose almost twice as much by missing game as by going one down. You should therefore bid "one more for game" when vulnerable on any reasonable hope, even if the success of the contract is slightly less than an even chance. Apart from the mathematical probabilities involved, there is always the possibility of a defensive error or favourable lead that presents you with the contract.

(c) Slams

A little slam is hardly worth bidding unless it is better than an even chance. In other words, a slam depending upon a finesse is not a particularly good propostion, whether vulnerable or not. The bid stands to lose about as many points as it stands to gain, e.g. Not Vulnerable.

You bid four spades and make twelve tricks	+ 480
Your opponents bid and made six spades	+ 980
Net loss = 500	
You bid six spades and go one down	- 50
Opponents bid four spades and make eleven tricks	+ 450
Net loss = 500	

Vulnerable, the difference is 750 in each case.

It might be fairly argued that, as the net gain or loss is the same, you might just as well bid the slam as not. Unless personal considerations (e.g. your opponents are known to bid slams freely) influence your decision, it is more probable that the other side will not have bid the slam. It is therefore preferable that the gain should be greater than the possible loss.

In addition to the points involved there is the effect on morale. A pair that goes down in a slam, uncertain whether the result will be the same in the other room, mentally records a loss of 500 or 750 points on the board and subconsciously tends to press to regain lost ground. Their successful opponents on the other hand, receive a boost to their morale which may well have the effect of improving their judgment on later hands.

In considering the approximate odds that should be accepted before bidding a small slam it has only been assumed that the two possible results are:

(a) slam made

(b) slam one down

but there is the added possibility that the slam is bid in the wrong suit. This occurred in a match on the following hand:

South Dealer
Love All

North
- ♠ J 10 6 5
- ♡ Q 10 8
- ◇ A 5 2
- ♣ Q J 3

West
- ♠ K 7
- ♡ 6 5 4
- ◇ Q J 10 3
- ♣ K 8 5 4

East
- ♠ 8 3 2
- ♡ 9 2
- ◇ 9 8 7 6
- ♣ 10 9 6 2

South
- ♠ A Q 9 4
- ♡ A K J 7 3
- ◇ K 4
- ♣ A 7

One team bid six hearts and had to go one down as both kings were on the wrong side. Their opponents reached the superior contract of six spades, which was made because the hearts provided discards for dummy's clubs. It could be claimed that the heart slam was unlucky as both finesses were wrong. The team lost 1030 (980 + 50) whereas had they not bid the slam at all the loss would have been 530 (980 − 450). In this example the loss was largely due to inferior bidding, but a similar swing could result where the success of the contract depends on a complete guess. Suppose the trump suit is:

K 9 6 5

A J 10 7 2

with one loser outside. If one team bids the slam and guesses wrong and their opponents bid it and guess right the loss is 1030 or 1530 depending on vulnerability. If the slam is not bid by the other team the loss is only 500 or 750.

A grand slam should never be bid in a match of 32 boards unless it is such a certainty that the contract can be claimed at the first trick. The defeat of a grand slam by one trick costs 1030 or 1530 depending on the vulnerability. The loss is the same as bidding a little slam in the wrong suit.

If you bid a grand slam in the wrong suit, or it depends on a guess and you are unlucky, the loss is over 1500 non-vulnerable and 2300 vulnerable. In a short match this size of loss is almost impossible to recover.

Sacrifice Bidding

The position as to whether to sacrifice or not is somewhat simplified by knowing exactly what the opponents stand to score if they make their contract. Provided that the loss is less than they would in theory have made you should show a profit.

The most important factor is whether they are sure to make their contract. It is most annoying to make a 'phantom sacrifice' whereby you incur a heavy penalty to save an unmakeable game. In attempting to give some guidance on this subject it is presumed:

(1) opponents are certain to make the contract

(2) that you have no hope of making yours,

(3) that you will be doubled.

(a)　At love all opponents will score approximately 420 points

　　　2 down = 300　　　　　You gain 120
　　　3 down = 500　　　　　You lose　80

At this score it is reasonably safe to sacrifice as the loss, even if you go 3 down, is comparatively small.

(b)　At game all opponents will score approximately 620

　　　2 down = 500　　　　　You gain 120
　　　3 down = 800　　　　　You lose 180

Here the loss due to a miscalculation is more serious and you should only save if you expect to go no more than one down, when you gain 420. It allows for a margin of error of one trick, when your gain will be 120.

(c)　Opponents only are vulnerable. Opponents will score approximately 620.

　　　2 down = 300　　　　　You gain 320
　　　3 down = 500　　　　　You gain 120
　　　4 down = 700　　　　　You lose　80

This is the best position in which to make a sacrifice bid. Even an unexpected defeat by four tricks will cost only 80 points.

(d)　Your side only is vulnerable. Opponents will score approximately 420

　　　2 down = 500　　　　　You lose　80
　　　3 down = 800　　　　　You lose 380

Under these conditions you should only sacrifice when you are confident of being only one down at the most, with a faint possibility of making the contract.

Costly sacrifices against slams can only pay if your other pair has bid and made it. It is therefore advisable to:

Save a small slam at the cost of a game

Save a grand slam at the cost of a small slam.

To lose 1700 points to save a grand slam vulnerable (= 2200 approximately) is, on the face of it, a good proposition since you have saved 500. If, however, only a small slam is reached in the other room you have lost about 300.

Accepting a Sacrifice

Provided that you are certain to defeat the opponents and are uncertain of making a higher contract yourself it is better to double and thus ensure a plus score even though it does not fully compensate you for the loss of your game. For example, you are vulnerable and bid four spades and the opponents bid five clubs. They are not vulnerable and are clearly trying to sacrifice. Unless you are absolutely certain of making five spades you should double. If you collect 300 it is disappointing and you will lose 320, but if you collect 500 your loss is only 120.

But if you go five spades and go one down, possibly doubled, and game is bid and made in the other room, your loss is 820 (620 + 200). When the issue is in doubt and it is possible the opponents may make their contract and you may also make yours, then you should bid one more for safety. Competitive situations of this type are discussed under the heading of "Avoiding Big Swings" (page 53).

Personal Factor

Tactics cannot be governed solely by mathematical considerations. Knowledge of the opponents in the other room is important. If they are known to be bold bidders certain liberties must be taken. Apart from the make-up of the players other considerations may influence bidding tactics. For example, a team of inexperienced players is drawn against a team of acknowledged masters. It is not unreasonable in such circumstances for the lesser lights to 'shoot' and take reckless chances, for they have all to gain and little to lose.

If they are defeated by 9000 instead of 4000 it does not matter and, as they are outclassed, it is worth trying to bring off a coup. In these circumstances the restrictions advised about bidding grand slams can be relaxed a little. The most outrageous bluff may very well have electrifying results. These tactics will be even more likely to succeed if the masters make the stupid, but not uncommon, error of underestimating the opposition.

If you play against a team considerably weaker than yours bear in mind the possibility that the adversaries may go all out. At the same time treat the match as if it were the final of the Gold Cup. To do otherwise, besides being discourteous, is to lower your standard to that of your less experienced opponents.

All-out tactics are also to be expected from a team heavily down at half time. Let us suppose that in a thirty-two board match one side is 2500 down; it may decide to shoot every possible game, and slam, in the hope of bringing off a miracle. Such tactics are of doubtful value except in the most desperate situations and usually result in inflating the margin of defeat. The leading team should therefore adopt moderately bold tactics, ensuring that no vulnerable game is missed nor any even money slam. Grand slams should still only be bid when 3-1 on, since the loss of 750 (vulnerable) will not lose the match, but 1500 might.

It can be fatal for a team well ahead at half time to adopt safety first as their motto. A glaring example occurred in the Vanderbilt Cup 1952, one of the most important team events in U.S.A. A comparatively unknown team (certainly at that time) of Bishop, McHenry, Johnson and Clancy were drawn against the World Champions, Crawford, Becker, Stayman, Rapee and Schenken. After 24 boards the "unknowns", playing inspired bridge were deservedly 3770 points ahead. In the second half they decided to hold on to their lead by displaying the utmost caution. The World Champions adopted all-out tactics and recovered 6330 points in 24 boards, to win by 2560.

Avoid Big Swings

Since aggregate scoring is merely a matter of which side scores the most points, it is quite possible to win or lose a match on one hand. Reference has been made to the heavy loss that can result from an unsuccessful slam bid. The example quoted above illustrates what can happen as a result of ultra caution.

Care should be taken to avoid big swings. Risks should not be taken when the possible loss is out of proportion to the possible gain.

It is not worth risking doubling opponents into game for a one trick set. Nor is it wise, when vulnerable, to indulge in light protective or balancing bids. If, for example, the dealer on your left opens one spade, the next two players pass, and you hold;

♠ 8 6 5
♡ Q 7 2
◇ A 9 5
♣ K 9 6 2

pass. It is extremely unlikely that your side can make game and if you compete you may end up losing 500 when all you were likely to gain if all went well was about 200, representing a part score for you instead of them.

Part scores should certainly be contested, but not at the risk of heavy loss.

It is in the competitive situations that the biggest swings occur, when each side can make a game or even a slam. An oft quoted example is the following. It happened in a Gold Cup Final between Ingram and Lederer.

West Dealer
North-South Vul.

North
♠ 2
♡ Q J 9 8 4
◇ 10 5 4
♣ K 6 4 2

West
♠ A K Q J 10 8
♡ A 10 3
◇ Q J
♣ 5 3

East
♠ 9 7 5 3
♡ K 7 6 5 2
◇ -
♣ J 10 9 8

South
♠ 6 4
♡ -
◇ A K 9 8 7 6 3 2
♣ A Q 7

In one room East — West bid up to five spades doubled and made eleven tricks for a score of 750. In the other room North — South were doubled in six diamonds which was also made, scoring 1490, a net gain to Ingram's team of 2240 points. The scoring was in accordance with the laws at the time. As the match was won by 2300 points it can be seen that this hand was decisive. The moral is 'If in doubt bid one more'. It is safer than risking an enormous swing if a game or slam is made by the same team in each room.

Here is a further example from a teams match:

South Dealer
Game All

North
♠ 5 4
♡ K J 8 7 6
◇ 7 3
♣ K Q J 4

West
♠ Q 10 8 6 2
♡ 5 4
◇ J 9 8 6 4 2
♣ -

East
♠ A J 9
♡ Q
◇ A K Q 10 5
♣ 9 7 5 3

South
♠ K 7 3
♡ A 10 9 3 2
◇ —
♣ A 10 8 6 2

In one room East — West bid up to five spades and North — South, uncertain whether they could defeat them, bid six hearts. This contract was doubled for a score of 1660. In the other room East — West were doubled in five diamonds for a score of 750, a gain of 2410.

Here are the two further examples of large swings from American matches. The first occurred in the 1953 Vanderbilt Cup and resulted in the defeat of Crawford's team (Schenken, Becker, Stayman and Rapee) by a quartet from New York (P & J. Atiyeh, Perry and McChance) by 1860 points. The hand was reported in the *Bridge World*.

North Dealer
Game All!

                              North
                              ♠ 8
                              ♡ A Q J 10
                              ◊ K Q 9 6 4
                              ♣ Q J 7

West   East
♠ 7 3   ♠ 5
♡ 9 6 5 3 2   ♡ K 8 7 4
◊ 10 5   ◊ A J 8 3 2
♣ 9 4 3 2   ♣ A K 6

                              South
                              ♠ A K Q J 10 9 6 4 2
                              ♡ -
                              ◊ 7
                              ♣ 10 8 5

Bidding in Room One

S	W	N	E
		1 H	2 D
3 S	-	3 NT	-
4 S	-	4 NT	-
6 S	-	-	Dbl.

Reading the double as "Lightner" requesting a heart lead, West duly complied and ♡ 10 was covered by ♡ K and ruffed. Entering dummy with ♠ 8, South discarded his clubs on ♡ A Q J.

Bidding in Room Two

S	W	N	E
		1H	2D
4NT	—	5D	—
5S			

West led ◊ 10 taken by East. He thought the lead was singleton and returned the suit. South thought so too and ruffed high. He decided to play West for a singleton trump and crossed to the table with ♠ 8 and led ♡A, followed by ◊ K. West ruffed and returned a club for one down. Swing on the board 1760.

The second example occurred in the Summer Nationals 1953 and again the Crawford team was unfortunate.

West Dealer

North — South Vul.

<pre>
                    North
                    ♠ A Q 9 8 6 5
                    ♡ K 5
                    ◊ 5 4
                    ♣ K 7 3
West   East
♠ 10 7 2   ♠ 4 3
♡ -   ♡ A J 9 7 6 4 2
◊ J 10 9 8 6 2   ◊ Q
♣ J 8 5 4   ♣ 9 6 2
                    South
                    ♠ K J
                    ♡ Q 10 8 3
                    ◊ A K 7 3
                    ♣ A Q 10
</pre>

At one table West opened with a psychic one no trumps intending to retreat to diamonds, if necessary. Unfortunately the situation got out of control, his partner jumping to four hearts over North's spade intervention. This frolic cost 1100. The result would still have shewn a profit had their team mates reached six no trumps for this would have scored 1440. Alas! They reached the perfectly reasonable contract of 6 spades which was defeated by the lead of ace and another heart.

A more recent example of a large swing occurred in the Hubert Phillips Bowl, Mixed Teams Championship of the English Bridge Union. This is one of the few competitions in England with aggregate scoring.

North Dealer
North — South Vul.

                              North
                              ♠ A
                              ♡ K 10 7 4 3
                              ◊ A 10 8 7 5 3
                              ♣ 3

West   East
♠ 8   ♠ Q J 10 9 5 4 3 2
♡ A Q J 8 5 2   ♡ -
◊ Q J 4   ◊ K 9
♣ J 9 4   ♣ 8 5 2

                              South
                              ♠ K 7 6
                              ♡ 9 6
                              ◊ 6 2
                              ♣ A K Q 10 7 6

The bidding at both tables was,

S	W	N	E
		1 D	4 S
5 C	Dbl.		

Referring back to the subject of accepting a penalty, South should double 4 spades and be reasonably sure of a plus score.

At one table West led ♠8, won in dummy and a low diamond was led. East won and returned ♠Q ruffed by West, who returned ♡ A and ♡ Q ruffed by East. After a further spade ruff by West, East, having discarded ◊9 on ♡ A, trumped a diamond, declarer going four down for a loss of 1100 (or 1000 counting honours).

At the other table South, after winning the opening lead, played three rounds of trumps, discarding ♡ 3 and ◊3 from dummy. He next led ♡ 9, won by West who led back ♡Q to ♡ K. South next led ◊5 from the table, taken by East whose return of ♠Q was taken in hand with ♠ K. When declarer led out his remaining trumps. West had to find three discards from ♡ J 8 5 and ◊Q J, dummy holding ♡ 10 and ◊A 10 8 7. On the last trump he was squeezed and the contract made for a score of 850 (including honours) for a swing of 1850. The contract would have been defeated had East returned a diamond after winning with ◊K, for this would have removed the entry to the table and prevented the squeeze.

Weak – Strong No Trumps

There will always be arguments regarding the respective merits of the weak and strong No Trump.

The pre-emptive value of opening one no trump may result in preventing the opponents competing profitably in a suit. This is less likely with the development of counter measures such as Sharples, Astro etc.

This aspect will be examined in more detail in considering tactics in pairs competitions.

Vulnerable, the weak no trump is highly dangerous as it may result in a penalty of 800 or 1100. Although this loss may be reduced a little if your other pair can make a game, there is always the danger that game is not biddable or may fail. For example, you open one no trumps with 13 points, the next player doubles and all pass. Your partner contributes 2 points and no long suit. Having to play from your own hand all the time you may easily end up 3 or 4 tricks down, losing 800 or 1100. While it is true that the opponents with 25 combined points may make game, nevertheless it is not a certainty that game will be made and your other pair may have lost an additional 100 or even 200.

Apart from the mathematical considerations, the loss of a heavy penalty on so small a contract is disturbing to morale. It is therefore advisable to avoid playing the weak no trump vulnerable, certainly in aggregate competitions.

Play

It is rarely that a match governed by aggregate scoring is won by less that 300 points and therefore odd tricks are not of supreme importance. For this reason the achievement of the contract is the prime consideration of the declarer and defeating it is all important to the defenders. Safety plays are definitely advisable to ensure a contract even though they may concede a possible overtrick. For example, playing in four spades you have lost two tricks, and the only other possible losers are in trumps of which you hold

♠ A 10 6 4

♠ K 9 8 3 2

To ensure that only one trick is lost the standard play is to lead a low card from either hand and covering whatever card is played by the next player. Thus, if you lead ♠ 2 and West plays ♠ 5, play ♠ 10 from dummy (North). If East wins there are only two spades left and they are bound to fall to the ace and king. If West holds all four, ♠10 will win. If West shows out at the first lead you can restrict your loss to one trick by leading through East's ♠Q J 7 5. Had you played either ace or king on the first round and discovered a 4-0 split, it might be impossible to avoid the loss of two tricks.

Safety play gained 500 on this hand from a teams match
South Dealer
Love All

```
                          North
                          ♠ 7
                          ♡ 8 6 3
                          ◇ 5 4
                          ♣ A K J 7 5 4 3
West                                          East
♠ K 9 8 4 3                                   ♠ J 10 6 5
♡ K 7                                         ♡ Q J 9 2
◇ Q 8                                         ◇ K 10 7 6 2
♣ Q 10 9 8                                    ♣ -
                          South
                          ♠ A Q 2
                          ♡ A 10 5 4
                          ◇ A J 9 3
                          ♣ 6 2
```

The contract at each table was three no trumps by South and the lead was ♠4. One declarer, after winning with ♠Q led ♣6 and finessed ♣J when West played ♣10. He was perfectly correct in not playing out ♣A K hoping for an even break, for this would be too great a gamble. But when East showed out, it was impossible to prevent West from blocking the run of the clubs and the contract was two down (-100).

At the other table the declarer was extra careful. He led ♣6 and West played ♣10, and ♣2 was played from dummy. When East discarded it was a simple matter, after regaining the lead, to lead ♣2 and finesse ♣J and capture both West's remaining clubs with ♣A K.

Had East followed to the first round of clubs, there would be only two outstanding, which must fall to the ace and king. This situation is clear cut in aggregate as the loss of a possible unnecessary trick is of little consequence compared with the achievement of the contract.

In pairs, where every trick counts, it is a difficult decision as will be explained in a later chapter.

Such safety plays may savour of a pessimistic outlook, but they are essential in a contract where the loss of 600 or more points can be prevented at the cost of a mere 30 (i.e. one overtrick).

Risks may also be taken in defence since the points that may be gained by the defeat of a contract are far more than the cost of a possible overtrick if a gamble fails.

For example you are South defending 4 spades after this auction —

S	N
1 S	3 C
3 S	4 S

You hold ♠ 7 4 2, ♡ K 2, ◊ J 8 5 4 and ♣ 8 7 4 3. It is a fair gamble to lead ♡ K. As the opponents have not tried for a slam your partner probably holds an ace. If it should be the ace of hearts you may get a ruff. That is three tricks and one may turn up from a losing finesse or the equivalent. Of course you may give declarer an extra trick, but it is unlikely to be the tenth trick; more probably an overtrick.

If you find yourself in a speculative contract chances must be taken in an endeavour to make it, even though by doing so you may go down more than you need. Assume you have reached six no trumps on the following:

```
        ♠  5 2
        ♡  7 6 3
        ◊  A K J 9 7 6
        ♣  7 5


        ♠  A 4 3
        ♡  A K 8 2
        ◊  10 8
        ♣  A K Q 6
```

West leads ♠ K. Clearly the diamond finesse must succeed and you cannot afford to lose more than one trick. You must therefore win the second trick and finesse diamonds at once. This is the correct percentage play which caters for West holding Q x x or Q x x x. If the finesse loses a spade will probably be returned and you may well be four down. You could, of course, probably ensure making nine tricks, possibly ten, by holding up the ace of spades until the third round but this would be defeatist. The loss of an extra 100 points or so is negligible compared with the bonus for making the slam.

If you are doubled and vulnerable the position may be different. It is likely that your opponents will bid and make three no trumps for a score of 600. If you go four down and lose 1100 you have lost 1700 in all.

If you hold up♠A and later finesse diamonds, playing for nine tricks you lose 800, or 500 if you make ten tricks. If you take the second spade and cash eight tricks you lose 1100. There is a small chance of finding◇Q doubleton on your right but all in all you may as well play for the contract as it will not be so much more expensive if it fails. But if you make the doubled slam you score 1680 and gain 1000. Consider a further example. By bold bidding you reach three no trumps vulnerable on the following collection:

♠ 2
♡ Q 5 4
◇ Q 7 3
♣ K 6 5 4 3 2

♠ A K 7 4
♡ A 10 3
◇ 8 6 2
♣ A 10 8

The opening lead is a small diamond and the defence take the first four tricks and switch to ♠Q. The point is:

(a) Should you go all out for the contract?

(b) What should you discard from hand on the fourth diamond?

If the answer to the first question is "Yes", you must discard a small club and later play out ace and king, hoping for a 2-2 split. Unless you discard your third club the suit will be blocked. If the clubs fail to break evenly you will probably be four down, losing 400. On the other hand, if you play safe and concede a club trick early, you will be likely to make eight tricks and be only one down, losing 100. If you are not doubled you should adopt a 'sink or swim' policy. If you are doubled and North elects not to retreat to the comparative safety of ♣4 you should play for one down unless your position is desperate and you need points badly. Otherwise you stand to lose 1100 which is too much, particularly as it is most improbable that the other side will be in three no trumps.

Psychology

Keep in mind the player occupying your position in the other room. He plays the same cards as you do. Avoid the error made by a certain expert. Drawn against an inexpert team, the masters were about 1500 up at half-time. During the second half a hand arose which was bid to a small slam in both rooms. The success of the contract depended on either a simple finesse or a squeeze. The expert played for a squeeze and failed as the essential cards were not in the same hand. The less experienced player knowing nothing of squeezes took the finesse and won.

A similar situation occurred quite recently. Both teams were in three no trumps. One declarer, an acknowledged master player, contrived a brilliant line of play that was calculated to make the contract if a certain king was badly placed. Unluckily the king in question was right and the contract was defeated for a big swing. His less ingenious and exalted counterpart took an obvious finesse and wrapped up nine tricks.

If your team is well up your main consideration should be to avoid unnecessary adverse swings, either through bidding or play. If a guess has to be made try to adopt the line that you think your opponent at the other table will take, so that if you fail so also will he.

If you are down and need a swing in your favour, you may have to play against the odds in order to achieve a different, and you hope better, result than your adversary.

6

TEAMS OF FOUR
INTERNATIONAL MATCH POINTS

The essential difference between aggregate and match point scoring is that with the latter it is virtually impossible to win or lose a match on one hand. The largest total of IMPS that can be gained on one hand is 25 for which a swing of 3500 is required. A vulnerable game swing represents 12 or 13 IMPS, e.g. four spades bid made at one table = 620 and the same contract defeated at the other = 100. Total 720 = 12 IMPS. If an overtrick had been made at one table the difference would be 650 + 100 = 750 = 13 IMPS. Two such swings will yield 24 or 25 points and recover the huge loss of 25 resulting from a gain to one team of 3500 on one hand.

A series of gains on part scores will also mount up. Suppose one team bids and makes two spades (110) in one room, playing North – South, and their other half bid and make three clubs at the other table, scoring a further 110, the total gain is 220 = 6 IMPS. If this occurs four times in a match the total gain is 24 IMPS, practically equal to the amount gained for 3500.

When discussing tactics at aggregate scoring it was pointed out that part scores, whilst important, were not worth the taking of great risks. The loss of 200 on a part score is unlikely to decide the match. But a rash overcall costing 500 represents about two and a half times as much. With IMPS the difference is less: failing to enter the bidding and allowing your opponents to make a part score in both rooms may cost 220 = 6 IMPS. An unlucky overcall which loses 500 costs 11 IMPS, less than twice as much. As your team mates should be able to score 100 points or so on their cards your loss is around 400 = 9 IMPS; only three points more than you would have lost by not competing. This does not mean that you should overcall rashly but merely points out that part scores may prove to be more costly with IMP scoring than with aggregate.

Non-vulnerable games should be bid on an even money chance

(a) Non-vulnerable you bid three spades making ten tricks.

                                                          Score 170 points

    Opponents bid four spades, making ten tricks   Score 420 points

               Gain to opponents 250 = 6 IMPS

(b) You bid four spades, making nine tricks   Score - 50

    Opponents bid three spades, making nine tricks   Score + 140

               Gain to opponents 190 = 5 IMPS

There is not very much in it.

But vulnerable games should be bid on less favourable odds as the possible gain is greater.

(c) Vulnerable you bid three spades, making ten tricks.   Score 170

    Opponents bid four spades making ten tricks   Score 620

               Gain to opponents 450 = 10 IMPS

(d) You bid four spades making nine tricks   Score -100

    Opponents play in part score, making nine tricks   Score 140

               Gain to oppenents 240 = 6 IMPS

Their bidding and making a game not reached by the opponents wins 10 IMPS, but going one down when the other side stop in a part score only loses 6 IMPS.

In the case of a small slam the points won and lost through either missing or going down are equal, e.g:

Opponents bid six spades and you stop in four spades making twelve tricks

              They gain 500 = 11 IMPS Not vulnerable

              They gain 750 = 13 IMPS Vulnerable

If you go down one trick in six spades and opponents stay in game making eleven tricks you lose

            500 (450 +   50) = 11 IMPS Not vulnerable

            750 (650 + 100) = 13 IMPS Vulnerable.

Since bidding a slam involves a certain amount of risk the possible gain is not sufficient to justify calling a small slam when the chances are not better than even. For, if the slam is doubtful, it is by no means certain that the other side will bid it.

Bidding a slam in the wrong suit or going down on a blind guess is less expensive in IMPS than in aggregate, e.g.

Not Vulnerable

Opponents make six spades. You are one down. Loss 1030 = 14 IMPS
Opponents make six spades. You stay in four spades.

Loss   500 = 11 IMPS

In aggregate the loss in the case of an unsuccessful slam is twice as much as if you had not bid it. But in IMPS the difference is only 3 IMPS.

Vulnerable

Opponents make six spades. You are one down.

Loss 1530 = 17 IMPS

Opponents make six spades. You stay in four spades.

Loss   750 = 13 IMPS

In aggregate the loss in the case of an unsuccessful slam is again twice as much as missing it but the difference in IMPS is only 4. Grand slams should still only be bit when success is virtually assured. Although the defeat of a grand slam is not quite such a disaster at match points as in aggregate, the loss is still greater than the possible gain.

(a) *Not-vulnerable* you bid six spades. Opponents bid seven spades
    Net loss 500 = 11 IMPS

(b) You bid seven spades and go one down and opponents bid and make six spades.
    Net loss 1030 = 14 IMPS

(c) *Vulnerable* you bid six spades. Opponents bid seven spades.
    Net loss 750 = 13 IMPS

(d) You bid 7 spades and go one down and opponents bid and make six spades
    Net loss 1530 = 17 IMPS

Unless the opponents are known to be bold bidders it is problematical whether they will bid the grand slam. In addition to the mathematical considerations all the personal factors mentioned in connection with aggregate scoring apply. Defeat in a slam, whether little or big, is apt to have a depressing effect and lead to "pressing" on future hands to recover the loss with disastrous consequences.

Finally, if you bid a grand slam in the wrong denomination, or it depends on a two way finesse and you guess wrong and the others guess right, the result is a loss of 2310 (seven spades) or 20 IMPS. Had you been content with a little slam your loss would only be 750 or 13 IMPS.

Sacrifice Bidding

Against Games

It is difficult to assess accurately the likely gain or loss from deliberately overbidding to save game, since you may go either more or fewer tricks down than you expected. Examining the possibilities it is assumed in each case:

(i) that there is no hope of you making your contract
(ii) that you will be doubled
(iii) that the opponents' contract will succeed.

Love All Opponents bid four spades and you bid five clubs

2 down = 300	You save 120	=	3 IMPS
3 down = 500	You lose 80	=	2 IMPS

The prospects for sacrificing are reasonable. You stand to gain 3 IMPS if your judgment is right and lose only 2 IMPS if you are wrong to the extent of one trick. In addition there is the possibility that you push the other side one too high or that you go one less down, in which latter event you gain 320 = 8 IMPS.

Game All. Opponents bid four spades and you bid five clubs

2 down = 500	You save 120	=	3 IMPS
3 down = 800	You lose 180	=	5 IMPS

Here the loss if your judgement is wrong is greater than the likely gain. If you are only one down for 200 your gain is 9 IMPS (620 - 200 = 420).

Opponents Vulnerable They bid four spades and you bid five clubs

2 down = 300	You save 320	=	8 IMPS
3 down = 500.	You save 120	=	3 IMPS
4 down = 700.	You lose 80	=	2 IMPS

This is the best position for sacrifice bidding. You gain tremendously if you are only two down and still shew a profit if you are 3 down. Even if things go badly and you are four down, you only lose 2 IMPS.

At this score there is a fair chance that opponents may bid one more. If this should prove too much for them you stand to gain 12 IMPS (620 + 100 = 720).

Your Side only Vulnerable. Opponents bid four spades and you bid five clubs

2 down = 500.	You lose 80	=	2 IMPS
3 down = 800.	You lose 380	=	9 IMPS

This is quite the worst position in which to sacrifice. At the score there is little chance that they will bid higher. You should only sacrifice if you are certain that you will go at most one down and that there is a sporting chance of making your contract.

B. Against Slams

On the face of it, it would seem that fantastic sacrifices would prove worth while against a slam. If the opponents are standing to make anything between 1000 and 2000 points you can afford to go down a good many tricks and still show a profit.

The snag in this argument lies in the fact that your other pair may fail to reach the slam. It may depend on a finesse or be too difficult to bid.

In a recent County match one pair outbid six hearts with seven clubs and lost 1100. As the opponents were vulnerable they would have scored 1430 had they succeeded in their contract so the save appeared to be worthwhile. Unfortunately the slam was not bid at the other table so the sacrifice cost 420 (1100 - 680 = 420) representing 9 IMPS. Had they not saved and the slam had been made they would have lost 13 IMPS. But the slam was not a certainty so it would have been better to take a chance of defeating it.

The following is a reasonable yardstick:

To save a small slam the sacrifice should not greatly exceed the value of a game.

To save a grand slam the sacrifice should not exceed the score for a small slam.

Example 1. Love All

Opponents bid six spades. You can afford to sacrifice if your maximum defeat is three tricks, amounting to 500. This is not much in excess of the score for game. If your other pair do not bid the slam they will probably score 450 or 480 and your loss is either 1 or 2 IMPS.

If the slam is bid and made at the other table you gain 480 = 10 IMPS. Suppose you go five down and lose 900. In theory this is cheaper than the slam.

If your other pair stop in game, you lose 420 - 9 IMPS.

If your other pair stop in game and you do not save you lose 500 = 11 IMPS.

If your other pair bid and make a slam you gain 80 = 2 IMPS.

Example 2. Opponents Vulnerable. They bid seven spades.

You can afford to go down as many as 7 or 8 tricks for the penalty of 1300 or 1500 is about the same as the score for a small slam (1430).

Thus if your other pair bid and make six spades and you lose 1300 you gain 130 = 4 IMPS. If you go down 1500 you lose 2 IMPS. But before indulging in such a save be convinced that there is no likelihood of the contract being made. It may take very little to upset a grand slam.

Accepting a Sacrifice

The old adage "half a loaf is better than no bread" is true and in most cases it is advisable to make sure of a plus score by accepting a reasonable penalty rather than risk being pushed too far and ending up with a minus.

Example 1. Love All.

You bid four hearts and opponents save in four spades

If you double and score 300 you lose 120	=	3 IMPS
If you double and score 500 you gain	=	2 IMPS
If you bid five hearts and go one down you lose 470	=	10 IMPS
If you are doubled the loss is 500	=	11 IMPS

Example 2. Game All.

You bid four hearts and opponents bid four spades

If you double and collect 500 you lose 120	=	3 IMPS
If you double and collect 800 you gain 180	=	5 IMPS
If you bid five hearts and go one down you lose 720	=	12 IMPS
If you are doubled the loss is 820	=	13 IMPS

If the opponents sacrifice against your slam bid there is little you can do except double, even if the penalty is paltry compared with what you were going to score. You have been deprived of the chance of scoring the full value of your cards and failure to appreciate the fact may be costly.

A notable instance arose in the Tollemache Cup – Inter Regional Teams Championship of the English Bridge Union. A London pair bid to seven diamonds without intervention. Seeing no defence to this a Kent pair bid seven spades holding nothing at all except six or seven headed by the queen. As seven diamonds stood to score 2140, being vulnerable, it was most unlikely that the non-vulnerable sacrifice of seven spades would go down a comparable amount as an eleven trick defeat would be needed. The London player therefore bid seven no trumps. This went one down so the team lost 100 in addition to the score for the small slam bid and made at the other table. Clearly it would have been better to have taken the penalty, especially as the grand slam was not reached at the other table.

Personal Factor

A weak team opposed to a strong team may well adopt 'do or die' tactics in the hope of bringing off a miracle. But at IMP scoring they will need much more luck, for a bid swing on one hand will not be decisive as it might in aggregate. Suppose, for example, the inexperienced team big a vulnerable grand slam and make it with the help of three successful finesses and an even break in trumps; the expert team play the same hand in game and lose 1500 on balance. With aggregate scoring this would be a large amount to recover, but at IMP scoring the loss on the board would be 17 IMPS. This could be neutralized by one game scoring 12 and one part score 6.

For this reason it is more than ever important that the stronger team should play steadily throughout and depend on their superior skill to carry them through. Unnecessary pressing to get back lost points is not advisable as these can easily be recovered on quite ordinary looking hands.

One frequently hears a team which is down 20 IMPS or so with one set of boards to play remark that they hope for some big hands. But big hands are not really necessary, for they are not the only ones that can create big swings.

Suppose that on each of the eight boards North – South held 27-28 points between them. There will probably not be many big differences in the score because there is enough to make a game easy to reach and the only difference is likely to be one or two overtricks, representing 1 or 2 IMPS. But a series of hands with a combined count of 24 or 25 is much more likely to produce a big turnover as game may be bid at one table and not at the other, and also made in one room and defeated in the other.

Even with part score hands, where the high card strength is evenly divided steady gains of 160 (two spades made in one room and defeated in the other) and 220 (part score made in both rooms) representing 4-6 IMPS respectively, mount up. In a recent league match, played in two halves of 16 boards, the score at half time was 3 IMPS to one team. By normal bidding and play this lead was later increased to 42. Admittedly the losers may not have played well but there were no freak hands and no slams.

Ultra cautious tactics when well ahead can be equally costly at IMPS as at aggregate.

Avoid Big Swings

The danger of losing a match on one board is not great. Referring back to the hands cited under Aggregate Scoring the swings, in terms of match points, would be only 19 or 20 IMPS. Two game swings would neutralise the loss. Nevertheless, every effort should be made to avoid a big turnover. It is rarely worth while to double the opponents in a part score in a major suit for a one trick set. Assume that you bid up to three hearts and they bid three spades. You think you can make three hearts but not four hearts. You should pass. If they go one down and you score 100 you may lose 1 IMP if you would have scored 140. Had you doubled and made 200 your gain would have been 60, or 2 IMPS. Should your double misfire and they score 730 (180 + 50 + 500) you have lost 590 = 11 IMPS, assuming your pair score 140 in the other room.

The high competitive situations are the most difficult and here, as in aggregate, the best policy is, if in doubt bid one more. You may make it or you may push the opposition just one too high. The margin of loss, in any case, is likely to be less.

Example. Love All.

You bid four hearts and opponents bid four spades. You now have the choice of doubling, passing or bidding five hearts.

(i)   If you double and they make it, but you could have made five hearts you have lost   590   (240 + 50 + 300)

                                     450   (150 + 300)

                               1040   = 14 IMPS

(ii) If you bid five hearts and go one down doubled and they would have made four spades you gain 320 (420-100) = 8 IMPS

(iii) If you bid five hearts and go one down doubled, but four spades would have failed by one trick, you lose 200 (100 + 100) = 5 IMPS

(iv) If you double four spades and they make it and you would have been one down in four hearts, you have lost 490 (590-100) = 10 IMPS

By going one more you have minimized the risk of a big swing which might result from faulty judgment.

It is an interesting fact about IMP scoring that if each half of a team has a disaster, it is better that the disasters should occur on the same board.

Assume Team A is playing against Team B. North – South Vulnerable. On the second board the North – South half of team A doubles the opponents in two spades which is made, whereas North – South could have made three no trumps. The loss on the board is:

Room 1	470 (two spades doubled)
Room 2	600 (three no trumps made)
	1070 = 14 IMPS

On board 7 – Game All – the East – West half of team A bids six no trumps going one down, when six hearts is unbeatable. In the other room six hearts is duly bid and made. The loss is:

Room 1	1430 (six hearts bid and made by team B)
Room 2	100 (six no trumps one down by team A)
	1530 = 17 IMPS

These two boards have cost team A 31 IMPS. Had the disasters occurred on the same hand, i.e. instead of bidding and making six hearts team A doubled team B (non vulnerable) in two spades the loss would be

1430
 470

1900 which amounts to 18 IMPS

Had both sides been vulnerable so that two spades doubled scored 670, the total loss would be 2100 or 19 IMPS, certainly cheaper than 31.

Before leaving the question of big swings, here are two examples from international matches and one from an inter-county championship final. The first occurred in the Ireland — Portugal match in the 1973 European Championships in Ostend and resulted in a double slam swing.

Dealer East
Love All

North
♠ —
♡ K J 9 6 5 2
◊ —
♣ A Q J 8 6 4 2

West
♠ A K Q 7 5 3
♡ 7
◊ 9 8 7 4
♣ 10 3

East
♠ J 8 6 4
◊ 10 4
◊ A K Q J 6 5 3
♣ —

South
♠ 10 9 2
♡ A Q 8 3
◊ 10 2
♣ K 9 7 5

With Ireland sitting East — West in the open room the bidding proceeded

S	W	N	E
			1 D
—	1 S	2 D	4 S
5 H	5 S	6 H	6 S
Dbl.			

North led ♣ A and all thirteen tricks were made for a score of 1310.

In the closed room with Ireland North — South the bidding was

S	W	N	E
			1 D
—	1 S	Dbl.	2 S
3 H	4 S	6 H	Dbl.

West did not find a club lead so that all thirteen tricks were again made for a similar reward of 1310.

At first when the scores were announced the result was thought to be a "flat board", i.e. that the result was similar in each room with no swing. But it was soon realized that the Irish had made a slam in both rooms and gained 2620 or 21 IMPs. One can only conjecture on what would have happened if the policy of "if in doubt bid one more" had been adopted. If North — South had bid seven hearts they might have made it and scored 1770 if doubled, instead of losing 1310. Similarly if six spades had been called over six hearts in the closed room Portugal might have made 1310 instead of losing it.

The next case occurred in a match between Brazil and U.S.A in the 1970 World Championship in Stockholm. This is an example of bidding the wrong slam and being defeated through bad luck.

North Dealer
Love All

<table>
<tr><td></td><td>North
♠ A J 7 3
♡ J 10 8 7 6
◇ A
♣ 7 5 4</td><td></td></tr>
<tr><td>West
♠ —
♡ A 3
◇ K 9 8 7 4 3 2
♣ A Q J 8</td><td></td><td>East
♠ 10 9 6 2
♡ —
◇ Q 10 5
♣ K 10 9 6 3 2</td></tr>
<tr><td></td><td>South
♠ K Q 8 5 4
♡ K Q 9 5 4 2
◇ J 6
♣ —</td><td></td></tr>
</table>

The outcome of the hand and the resultant large swing depended on bidding style, whether you open one heart or one spade as South.

In the closed room with Brazil sitting North — South the bidding proceeded

S	W	N	E
		—	—
1 S	2 D	2 H	4 D
4 H	4 S	Dbl.	—
6 S	Dbl.		

Played in six spades by South, the lead of either of West's aces is fatal.

If ♡ A is led, East's void is revealed and the next heart is ruffed. If ♣ A is led South is forced to ruff and the 4-0 trump break wrecks the contract. To draw trumps results in South having none left in either hand, which he cannot afford as ♡ A has to be cleared.

In the open room with U.S.A. North — South the bidding was

S	W	N	E
		—	—
1 H	3 D	4 D	5 D
5 H	6 D	—	—
6 H	Dbl.		

If North is declarer in six hearts he is defeated by a spade lead, but as it was, played by South, there was no defence, and the U.S.A. gained 1210 in one room and 100 in the other for 16 IMPS.

The third example occurred in the inter-county championship for the *Daily Telegraph* Cup.

West Dealer
Game All

```
                        North
                        ♠ A Q 10 6 3
                        ♡ A 4 2
                        ◊ 9 4
                        ♣ 6 5 2
    West                                    East
    ♠ 9 8 5 4                               ♠ K 7 2
    ♡ 8                                     ♡ J 10 7 6 5 3
    ◊ 8 6 5                                 ◊ —
    ♣ A J 8 4 3                             ♣ K Q 9 7
                        South
                        ♠ J
                        ♡ K Q 9
                        ◊ A K Q J 10 7 3 2
                        ♣ 10
```

In one room the bidding was

S	W	N	E
	—	—	1 H
Dbl.	—	2 S	—
3 NT			

West led ♡ 8 and South claimed twelve tricks for 690. Had West led a club, as he might, East — West would have scored 100.

In the other room a spectacular auction proceeded

S	W	N	E
	—	—	1 H
4 NT	—	6 C	—
6 D	Dbl.	6 S	—
7 D	Dbl.	—	—
—			

South intended his bid of four no trumps to be a request for aces, believing that six diamonds would be a fair prospect if North held two and prepared to pass if North showed one. But North regarded his partner's call as the "Unusual No Trump" convention indicating a minor two suited hand.

Regarding his hand as better than it might be with two aces North made the imaginative response of six clubs. South removed to six diamonds doubled by West who was proud of his club holding.

North now took the view that South must hold a strong diamond — spade hand and removed to six spades. This further unwelcome development forced South to correct to seven diamonds, again doubled by West.

Picturing North with five or six clubs headed by K Q and South void, West did not lead ♣ A which would have immediately defeated the slam. He led ♡ 8. South won in hand and drew trumps. Placing ♠ K on his right he led ♠ J to ♠ A and returned ♠ Q, ruffing out ♠ K and making his grand slam for a score of 2330 — a net gain of 17 IMPS.

Had West cashed ♣ A and gained 200, his team would have scored a total of 890 (690 + 200) and gained 13 instead of losing 17, a turnover of 30 IMPS. Had West led a club against three no trumps and scored 100, his team would have gained 2430 = 20 IMPS, only a difference of 3 IMPS from the actual result.

If West had led a club at the first table and ♣ A at the second, the difference on the board would have been a mere 100 = 3 IMPS.

Weak No Trumps

Since one isolated catastrophe is unlikely to be fatal a stronger case can be made out for the weak no trump. The pre-emptive value of the opening frequently prevents the opponents getting into the bidding and results in part score swings. The effectiveness of the weak no trump is less than it was owing to the various defensive counter-measures devised. Opening one no trump frequently results in missing a superior part score contract in a major suit but this is less of a disadvantage in teams than in pairs as the possible loss of a point is not important.

It is obviously important to consider the position if the opening bid is doubled and defeated. Suppose you only are vulnerable and go four down for 1100. It is probable that opponents can make game. If they are not vulnerable then game is worth 400 so that the loss is 700 or 12 IMPS.

If opponents are also vulnerable their game will score 600, reducing the deficit to 500 = 11 IMPS. If you go down 800 and opponents could have made 400 you lose 400 (9 IMPS) on balance. At game all the loss is only 200 (800-600) = 5 IMPS. The chief danger here is that game is not makeable on the opposite cards.

If you go down 500 an adverse game is by no means certain, in which case the loss is likely to be in the region of 360 (500-140) = 8 IMPS. To play the weak no trump vulnerable can be costly, but the occasional disaster may be offset by a couple of part score gains.

Not vulnerable the situation is more favourable. If you go four down (700) the loss is only 100 (3 IMPS) if opponents have a vulnerable game, and 300 (7 IMPS) if they are not vulnerable. If you lose 500 you gain 100 having saved a vulnerable game and lose 100 if opponents are not vulnerable.

Play

Generally speaking the achievement of the contract is the main consideration, particularly with games and slams. A safety play that stands to lose a trick is worth making, for one match point is a small price to pay to ensure against the loss of 10-12 points if game is lost through a bad break.

A gain of 13 IMPS resulted from a safety play made by Mrs Jane Priday on this hand from Great Britain's match against Netherlands in the Womens European Championships in Oslo 1969.

South Dealer
Game All

```
                        North
                        ♠ A Q
                        ♡ A Q 10 8 4 3 2
                        ◊ 7 5
                        ♣ J 3
        West                            East
        ♠ 8 5 4 3                       ♠ J 9
        ♡ J 9 6                         ♡ K
        ◊ A J 9 6                       ◊ 10 8 3
        ♣ 10 7                          ♣ A Q 9 6 5 4 2
                        South
                        ♠ K 10 7 6 2
                        ♡ 7 5
                        ◊ K Q 4 2
                        ♣ K 8
```

With Great Britain North – South in the open room the bidding was

S	W	N	E
-	-	1 H	2 C
2 S	-	4 H	-
-	-		

East led ♣ A and followed with a second club. With a top loser in diamonds it was essential to restrict the losers in trumps to one.

Mrs Priday made the standard safety play, leading ♡ 5 and playing ♡A from her own hand. This was rewarded when ♡K fell from East. This was not just a lucky shot. Had East also played a low card, there would be only honours left. After entering dummy with a diamond, to lead the last trump an honour would be certain to appear from West, unless East had started with K J x, in which case nothing could be done. As it was, after ♡K fell it was easy to finesse against ♡J and make eleven tricks.

In the closed room, North opened four hearts and all passed. The Dutch declarer finessed ♡Q on the first round and lost to ♡K. Later she played ♡ A but failed to drop ♡J and went one down.

It is true that if West had held ♡K x the safety play would have lost one trick and one point. But as it gained 13 IMPs there can be no doubting that good technique was rewarded.

The position regarding part scores may be more difficult. Suppose you are in two spades, on these hands

> ♠ Q 5
> ♡ A 7 3
> ◇ 9 5 2
> ♣ 10 6 4 3 2
>
> ♠ K J 10 9 7 4
> ♡ K J 5 2
> ◇ 8
> ♣ A 7

There is no real risk of defeat, for you must surely make 5 spades, 2 hearts and 1 club. You should, therefore, try for 4 heart tricks by leading ♡A and finessing ♡J in the hope that East holds ♡Q x x. If this succeeds you will make ten tricks, but it is unlikely that game will be bid at the other table as you only have 18 high card points between you. On the other hand, if opponents have bid up to three diamonds and pushed you to three spades, the situation is different. You must now try to ensure 3 tricks in hearts. The safety play is to lead ♡3 to ♡K and return ♡2 to ♡A, followed by ♡7 towards ♡J. This safeguards against finding a doubleton queen with West.

Here is another example

♠ A 9 7 4
♥ K 4 2
♦ 10 7 6
♣ A 4 3

♠ K 10 8 5 2
♥ A Q 7
♦ 9 8 2
♣ K 5

As South you open one spade and pass your partner's invitational raise to three spades. Opponents cash three diamonds and switch to a club. You should make the safety play in trumps to provide against a 4-0 trump break, by leading low from either hand and merely covering if the next player follows suit. For one thing you cannot afford to go down. For another there is the possibility that your adversaries may have bid to game in the other room. If the trumps are evenly divided you are bound to lose on the board, but if they are not you will gain, providing you do not go down yourself.

If you find yourself in a highly speculative contract, it will usually pay to go all out to make it unless doubled. Consider the following:

♠ 3
♥ 7 4 3
♦ A K 8 5 4 3 2
♣ 9 8

♠ A 9 7
♥ A 6 5
♦ J 6
♣ A J 6 5 2

Assume you have reached three no trumps, opponents having bid spades. West leads ♠4 and East plays ♠J. If the diamonds split 2-2 you make your contract with an overtrick. If not, you may well be four down. It is doubtful whether the other side will be in the same contract. More likely they will be in three diamonds which they will make. You can either gamble on the diamonds breaking and risk a four trick defeat, or play for one off by ducking a diamond. It appears from the lead that West holds five spades and East four, so that you will gain little or nothing by holding up and risk a switch to hearts. If not vulnerable and not doubled you should gamble. If you go one down and three diamonds or four diamonds is scored in the other room you will lose 4 or 5 IMPS. If you go four down (200) your loss is 310 or 330 representing 7 or 8 IMPS. But if you are lucky and score 430 whilst 130 is scored in the other room you gain 7 IMPS. Vulnerable, playing for one down loses in all 210 or 230 depending on whether opponents make 9 or 10 tricks in diamonds, i.e. 5 or 6 IMPS. If you go four down your loss is 510 or 530 = 11 IMPS in either case. If you are successful and score 630 you gain 500. It would therefore appear reasonable to take a chance whether vulnerable or not as you stand to gain 11 IMPS instead of accepting an almost certain loss of 5.

If you are doubled you cannot really afford to risk 700 or 1100 unless the situation is desperate. There is always the hope that your other pair may have bid up to three spades and made 140, the diamonds being 3-1.

A good example of seizing the only real chance of making a speculative contract is this one from the Ireland v Portugal match in the European Championships in Oslo 1969.

North Dealer
East-West Vul.

```
                     North
                     ♠ K 10 9 3
                     ♡ A 7
                     ◊ A K Q 2
                     ♣ Q 9 6
West                                    East
♠ 7 6 2                                 ♠ J 5 4
♡ J 5 3                                 ♡ K 10 9 8 4
◊ 9 3                                   ◊ 10 8 6
♣ J 10 7 5 2                            ♣ K 8
                     South
                     ♠ A Q 8
                     ♡ Q 6 2
                     ◊ J 7 5 4
                     ♣ A 4 3
```

With Fitzgerald and Seligman sitting North – South for Ireland the bidding was brief and to the point

S	W	N	E
		1 D	-
3 NT	-	6 NT	-

Receiving the favourable lead of ♣ J, Seligman played for the only distribution that could help. Following with ♣ 6 from the table and winning with ♣ A he cashed four rounds of spades, discarding ♡ 2 from hand. He next played off his four diamonds, finishing in his own hand. Next he led ♣ 4 to which West followed with ♣ 2 and ♣ 9 drew ♣ K from East. Having only hearts left in his hand, East had to lead from ♡ K giving declarer the last three tricks with ♡ Q, ♡ A and ♣ Q.

7

PAIRS CONTESTS MATCH POINTS
BIDDING TACTICS

The technique required for match pointed pairs tournaments is quite different from that required for other forms of duplicate. The primary purpose is not to amass the greatest total score throughout the session but to gain the largest number of match points by doing well on each individual board.

Reference back to the travelling score sheet shown on page 39 will make it clear that it is sufficient for your result to be superior to the others by a mere 10 points. If there are seven tables and at six of these East – West have all played the hand in two spades, scoring 110, but at your table you, as North – South, have played the hand in three diamonds, going two down for the loss of 100, you would score a "top" and receive 12 match points because no-one with your cards has achieved a better result. Suppose on another board you get your opponents down 2000 – seven down doubled and vulnerable. At all the other tables your side, not vulnerable, have bid and made three no trumps, scoring 400. You again score a "top". The fact that on this occasion your score is 1600 points better than any other is irrelevant.

In considering successful tactics for this type of tournament it is necessary to bear in mind that you are competing against several other pairs, not just one team. You must adjust your bidding and play so that your result is likely to be superior to that achieved by at least half the other players in your line.

Bidding

Games, whether vulnerable or not, should be bid providing they represent a reasonable risk. It is not so much the amount you lose by missing game as the fact that your score is inferior to that of your rivals. If you bid a game that is a reasonable contract to be in, you should not get a poor result if it fails through ill luck, such as an unexpected ruff or a bad trump break. If the bid is reasonable other pairs are likely to be in the same contract and meet a similar fate.

Occasionally hands crop up which can be termed "under-bidders paradise". They stop in a part score and because every finesse is wrong and all the missing trumps are in one hand they just get home, while all the rational players have gone down in game. This, of course, is very irritating but it must be borne philosophically as in the long run the underbidders will meet with little success.

If game is doubtful it is better to be cautious. For example, you open one spade and partner responds three spades. You hold:

♠ K J 10 7 6
♡ K J 2
◊ Q J 8
♣ Q 4

You should pass. It is possible to construct hands within the limits of partner's response where game can be made. But it is far more likely that you will make nine tricks at the most. In a team event you might take a chance, especially vulnerable where the loss of 100 instead of 50 is a small price to pay compared with scoring 620. In a pairs tournament, however, you are not considering one opposing pair but several. If the decision whether or not to bid game is very close it is certain that many will not be in it. If no game can be made and you are the only one to bid it you stand to get a bottom score. If you play safe you should ensure at least an average score, and if you manage to collect an extra trick you may get a top.

Caution is usually advisable with slams. If you bid a slam and go down you are likely to get a bottom. If you miss a slam that makes there will probably be others who have done the same. Complete certainty is required before bidding a grand slam, for failure is sure to be a disaster with no points.

Naturally tactics in slam bidding must vary with the strength of the field. If the field is made up of strong players you can afford to bid a little slam or an even chance because it is likely that others will do the same. In less exalted company it is pointless as other pairs will not have aspired to anything beyond a game. Explaining in tedious detail the beautiful sequence you employed to reach a slam that failed only because of an unlucky finesse will hardly compensate you for the nought which represents your score on the board.

The paramount need for obtaining the best score on each hand has its effect on the bidding. Indeed, it is an undisputed fact that many unsound contracts are reached purely with the object of notching an extra ten points.

A difficult tactical problem is created by the fact that no trumps score ten points more than the major suits. Thus if exactly ten tricks are available either in spades or no trumps, those who play in the latter will gain a match point advantage. Consider this example from a pairs competition of Love All:

♠ A 10 6 3 2
♡ 6 4
♢ Q 7 4 3
♣ A K

♠ 4
♡ A K Q 7 5 3 2
♢ 6 3
♣ Q 7 6

There is little doubt that most people would agree that four hearts is the best contract for the two hands. But as the ace and king of diamonds happened to be with West, eleven tricks could be made either in hearts or no trumps. Consequently those who played in the inferior contract and were lucky scored 460 against 450. Game in no trumps could easily fail if the diamonds were badly placed or the hearts did not break, but neither contingency would seriously endanger a game contract in hearts.

From the foregoing it might appear that the key to success in match pointed pairs is to play every hand in no trumps. This is a common belief and also a fallacy. There are, of course, hands where an equal number of tricks can be made either in no trumps or a suit. But there are just as many, if not more, where this is not the case. Playing in a suit contract you have more control over the hand and there are also more ways by which you can take tricks, mainly through the value of a trump. So if it seems logical and sensible to play a contract in a major suit, do so. You will find numerous instances where those in no trumps score 400, but those in a major suit score 420. Or it may be 430 against 450 where an overtrick has been made.

The same arguments cannot be put forward with minor suits as the difference is too great. For example:

3 C or 3 D = 110	2 NT = 120
4 C or 4 D = 130	3 H or 3 S = 140

To obtain a good score in a minor suit it may be necessary to make two extra tricks. You should, therefore, only play in a minor suit if it is the only contract possible. It is for this reason that minor suit slams are frequently missed. Suppose your partner opens one diamond and you respond one spade and he rebids three no trumps, indicating a powerful all round hand of about 19 high card points. You hold:

> ♠ A J 7 6
> ♡ 8 4
> ◊ K 9 4 3
> ♣ K 6 2

A slam in no trumps is problematical as the combined total of points is about 30 and it usually requires 33 or 34 to make twelve tricks in no trumps. But a small slam in diamonds might well be possible if the hands fitted well. If you make a try with four diamonds you are virtually committed to a slam. As the hands will almost certainly produce ten or eleven tricks in no trumps, scoring 430-460 (non-vulnerable), to stop in five diamonds and make 400 or 420 will be a very bad result. You will probably get the same score in terms of match points that you would have obtained had you bid six diamonds and gone down. Thus, once you have by-passed three no trumps there is no point in playing in a minor suit below the level of six.

In the above example you can only afford to make a slam try of four diamonds over three no trumps if you have bidding machinery that enables you to stop at four no trumps if you decide a slam is not on.

Part Score Bidding

With match points scoring you cannot afford to be left out of the bidding with a fair hand. Allowing the opponents to make a modest contract of two hearts (110) when you could have made three diamonds, or even gone one down (- 50) may well result in a bottom score, just as much as if you had gone down 800. Should your result be inferior to all the others in your line it is immaterial whether the difference is 10 or 1000.

In the battle for part scores the opener has a big advantage. Not only is there a chance that he can buy the contract cheaply before the opponents have been able to enter the bidding, but there is the added factor of safety. This tactical factor makes it important to open light.

Suppose, for example, at Love All you hold:

♠ J 3
♡ K 10 9 8 6 2
◊ A Q 7
♣ 8 5

and decide to pass. Your left hand opponent opens one spade, your partner passes and two spades is bid on your right. It is highly dangerous to bid three hearts at this juncture. Even if you find your partner with a fair hand you have allowed the opponents to get together so you will probably be out-bid. You are much better off to open one heart at the outset.

Fourth player, after three passes, has a difficult decision. He can take the line of least resistance and pass and throw the hand in, but to score nothing on the board can result in a bottom, if a small plus score was available for your side. In these circumstances it is no use going to extremes and opening on what is obviously insufficient strength.

In borderline cases the possession of spades may influence your decision.

Holding

♠ K J 9 6 5
♡ A 10 2
◊ K 6 3
♣ 5 4

it would be in order to open one spade, not vulnerable, after three passes.

Should the bidding become competitive the side holding spades has the advantage in that they can outbid their opponents at the same level. With modest borderline hands that are balanced it is probably best to open with a weak no trump. This is not likely to run into much trouble as no other player appears to hold an opening bid. It is pre-emptive and may therefore prevent much competitive bidding. The advantages and otherwise of the weak no trump will be examined in greater detail later (see pages 106-9).

The urgency of contesting part scores has led to a general weakening of the strength needed for a take-out double. It is permissible to double on any hand that justifies taking some action but does not contain a biddable suit. Thus, not vulnerable, you can afford to double an opening bid of one diamond on:

(a) ♠ A J 7   (b) ♣ K 10 7 6
     ♡ K 9 8 6   ♡ Q J 8 3
     ◊ 3 2   ◊ 2
     ♣ K 10 8 3   ♣ K J 4 2

The risk of serious loss is not great, certainly less than the possibility of missing a part score or pushing opponents too high. The double of a major suit should be stronger as your partner is forced to call at the two level. If the opener's partner should redouble and your partner is unable to assist you will have to extricate yourself also at the two level. Therefore, the double of one spade requires a better hand than the double of, say one club or one diamond.

The double by a player who has previously passed can be made on distributional values, e.g:

S	W	N	E
-	1 H	-	1 S

It would be correct to double with

                        ♠ 3 2
                        ♡ 6 4
                        ◊ K Q 6 5
                        ♣ Q J 9 7 6

Alter the hand to

                        ♠ 3
                        ♡ 6 4
                        ◊ K Q 9 6 5
                        ♣ Q J 9 7 6

and it would be correct to call one no trump. This would be the Unusual No Trump convention suggesting a minor two suited hand. Having passed originally and with West's hand unlimited your overcall of one no trump cannot be strong containing around 16 points. It must be a distributional hand containing both minor suits and not many points.

A certain degree of protection is needed in the battle for part scores and the strength for a take-out double can be reduced quite a lot, particularly if there is strength in a major suit. For example, if one heart is passed round to you, double with:

♠ Q 10 8 6
♡ 4 3
♢ A 10 5
♣ K J 9 2

whether vulnerable or not. The loss of a part score at match points can be just as costly as losing an 800 penalty.

In deciding whether or not to protect keep in mind whether the opening bid was likely to have shut out your partner with a fair hand. For instance, the player on your left opens one spade, the next two players pass.

You hold:

♠ 5 3
♡ A 9 6 2
♢ Q 10 8 6
♣ A 10 3

It is just worth a double. Your partner may have some values but was unable to take action over one spade second to speak.

But care should be taken over protecting a minor suit on light values. For one thing it was less dangerous for your partner to overcall. For another there is the distinct possibility that the opponents may find a better contract if you re-open the bidding.

The following hand from a pairs tournament illustrates the point.
West Dealer
Game All

North
- ♠ 9 4
- ♡ A K 3
- ◊ 10 8 2
- ♣ Q 10 8 6 5

West
- ♠ K Q 7 3
- ♡ 10 7
- ◊ A Q 4
- ♣ A K 7 2

East
- ♠ J 10 8 6
- ♡ J 9 6 4
- ◊ J 5 3
- ♣ 9 3

South
- ♠ A 5 2
- ♡ Q 8 5 2
- ◊ K 9 7 6
- ♣ J 4

S	W	N	E
	1 C	-	-
Dbl.	1 S	-	-

West made three spades, scoring 140, whereas had he been left in one club he would have been lucky to make it. The reason why South's double is open to question is because North could quite easily have bid over one club had he wished. There was therefore less incentive for his partner to protect. Furthermore, it frequently happens that a player opens with a minor suit on a very strong hand in order to make it easier for his partner to bid at the one level on a weak hand. Protecting on light values gives the opener a second chance.

Reasonable chances must also be taken with suit overcalls, particularly not vulnerable. If the suit can be called at a cheap level it should be bid if it contains lead directing value. For example, not vulnerable, overcall one heart with one spade on

- ♠ A Q J 9 7
- ♡ 5 4
- ◊ 9 7 3
- ♣ 8 6 2

Apart from the fact that your bid may prevent the opponents from reaching game in no trumps, or possibly defeating them if they do, the lead of your suit may save overtricks.

In contesting the bidding, the question of vulnerability is most important. In the situations so far discussed, vulnerability has not mattered. The initial effort, e.g. take-out double does not need to vary greatly in strength. Direct suit overcalls are, of course, affected as they are more subject to an immediate penalty double.

Greater care is needed in the later rounds, especially when vulnerable, for a two trick defeat costing 200 is always a bad result. This loss represents more than the maximum part score (140). Only if an adverse game can be both bid and made is the loss of 200 justified.

Lack of caution resulted in a zero score on these hands from a pairs contest. North — South vulnerable.

♠ J 8 2
♡ A Q 7
♢ 8 5 3
♣ J 10 9 4

♠ Q 9 5 4
♡ 10 8 2
♢ K Q 10 7
♣ A K

South opened with a weak no trump (12-14) and the next two players passed. East competed with two hearts which was passed round to North who contested with two no trumps. On a heart lead the contract went two down (-200). North hoped the loss would be only 100 which would be alright if East could make two hearts (110). This was faulty reasoning. There was no certainty that East would make his contract. In any event the risk was too great as North knew that his side had little, if any, superiority in high cards. Actually South had a maximum no trump and many players would consider the hand too strong, containing, as it did, 14 points and two tens. Not vulnerable the risk would be reasonable as two down would be 100. It is unlikely that the contract would be doubled.

In saving part scores it is important to remember that you cannot afford to go down more than 100. If you lose 150 (three down not vulnerable) or two down vulnerable (200) you are almost certain to get a bad result, for the maximum part score is worth 140 (3S or 3H).

Sacrifice Bidding

Providing your judgment is good regarding the impossibility of defeating the adversary's contract and the number of tricks you are likely to go down, sacrifice bidding is relatively straightforward. You know what the opponents stand to make and therefore you know what you can afford to lose. If you keep within these limits you should get a good score. If you exceed them you get a bad one.

In team events sacrifice bidding is less important as the points saved may, or may not, matter. If by calling five diamonds over four hearts you can lose 500 instead of 620 you have saved 3 IMPS. Had you not saved it might not have mattered very much. Equally if, at love all, you bid four spades over four hearts and go three down doubled, losing 500, when you expected to go only two down (300) it is not disastrous; the loss is only 80, or possibly 50 if eleven tricks in hearts could be made.

In a pairs contest points saved are of vast importance. To save a vulnerable game at a cost of 500 may well be a complete top. To miscalculate by one trick and go down 500 against non-vulnerable opponents who would have scored only 420 or 450 will almost certainly be a bottom.

> At love all you can afford to go 2 down = 300
> At game all you can afford to go 2 down = 500
> Opponents only game, you can afford to go 3 down = 500
> Your side only game you can afford to go 1 down = 200
> In each case it is assumed you will be doubled.

Obviously opportunities for saving game are quite good when vulnerability is equal. With adverse vulnerability the greatest care must be taken. A two trick set in these circumstances is fatal. The margin for error is so slender that a save should only be attempted when there is a fair possibility of making the contract. The ideal conditions, of course, are when the opponents are vulnerable and you are not. You can afford to take great liberties. It is very difficult for them to decide whether, should they double you instead of bidding game themselves, the penalty will be adequate. For this reason it is sound tactics to make overcalls on very weak hands, providing they contain length in a suit and poor defensive strength.

With vulnerability in your favour you should overcall one diamond with one heart with

♠ 4 2
♡ A 10 7 6 4 2
♢ 6 3
♣ 9 7 2

or even one spade on

♠ Q J 10 6 4 2
♡ 5 4
♢ 8 7 6
♣ J 10

It is unlikely that you will be doubled at the one level but if you are you should not be too worried. You should with partner's hand scramble four tricks which means the loss of 500 compared with the score the other side could have made for a certain game and possible slam.

Suit overcalls at the one level are even less hazardous, with the introduction of sputnik or negative doubles.

Overcalls at the two level are also worth risking if the loss is likely to conform to the principle that the probable gain will exceed the possible loss. An example of tempting your opponent to double occurred in a pairs tournament where East, vulnerable, opened a strong no trump (16-18).

South overcalled with two hearts on

♠ 5 3
♡ Q 10 7 6 4 3 2
♢ J 8 6
♣ 2

West held a massive hand and greedily doubled. North put down a modest 4 points which included the knave of hearts, bringing the combined total of points to seven. South managed to get away with two down (-300).

The opponents evinced disappointment when they looked at the travelling score sheet and saw that the normal score for their side was 1430 for six spades or 1440 for six no trumps.

In overcalling on weak hands, mainly with a view to a later sacrifice, the advantage of holding a good spade suit is considerable. It means that you can outbid the other side at the same level, pushing them up all the time.

Sacrificing against a slam is more hazardous. For one thing your judgment needs to be more accurate; it is pointless to incur a large penalty when the slam could not have been made. Also it is a waste of courage and match points if no other pair reaches it. If they make it you are doomed anyway so it may be better to hope it goes down.

It is best to follow the yardstick given earlier and repeated here for convenience.

To save a small slam the penalty should not exceed the value of a game.

To save a grand slam the penalty should not exceed the value of a small slam. In theory, to go down 1100 when opponents can make 1430 for a vulnerable little slam in a major suit is a fine result. But it is rarely that a slam is bid at every table. To incur a huge penalty before the slam has been reached is even more risky. In a club pairs competition a player opened three spades at favourable vulnerability on

♠ Q 10 9 5 3 2
♡ 6 4
♦ J 7 3
♣ J 6

He was doubled and lost 900. As the cards lay the opponents could make six clubs. This did not make the result any better as the slam was far from lay-down and nobody bid it. Cases do occur from time to time when a large penalty proves to be worth while.

A spectacular example occurred in the British Bridge League Simultaneous Pairs Tournament some years ago. Clubs throughout England played 24 pre-dealt duplicated hands. On one hand at love all, South dealt and opened with a game forcing bid of two clubs, holding no less than 30 high card points. West, on his left, held this worthless collection:

♠ 7 4 3
♡ 7 4
♦ J 9 8 3 2
♣ 7 3 2

and decided to make a frivolous bluff bid of two spades. North held ♠ K 10 8 6 2 and about 7 or 8 points in all and doubled. This was an error as a double in this position should indicate a poor hand apart from some trumps and be a warning to partner not to go on. With 7 or 8 points facing a two club opening a slam is likely. West decided to stand his ground and never made a trick at all. He was therefore eight down losing 1500. As all the other North — South pairs had bid either seven spades or seven no trumps and scored 1510 or 1520 the gallant West scored a top.

This type of coup only happens once in a lifetime and the player was lucky in that the opponents had a grand slam which was so obvious as to be universally bid. His partner might so easily have turned up with some small contribution such as Q J x in some suit that would have reduced the penalty by one trick for 1300 and only a small slam could be made on the opposite cards.

Tactics in High Competitive Situations

When both sides are bidding to a high level a wrong decision cannot settle the fate of a match pointed pairs in the same way that it can an aggregate teams or one governed by IMPS. All it can do is to make the difference between a top or a bottom. Therefore, in close decisions it is probably best to follow the rule 'if in doubt bid one more'. You may make it or push the other side too high. One's judgment can so easily be wrong in such cases. When vulnerability is on your side and the possibility of having to sacrifice is great, it is important that support for partner's suit should be shown early.

Consider the following sequence, East — West only being game.

S	W	N	E
	1 S	2 D	3 S
-	4 S	-	-
5 D			

South is at fault. Over East's three spades he should bid four diamonds. It is wishful thinking to assume that West will not voluntarily advance to game. Once South has indicated some support he can leave the decision whether or not to sacrifice to his partner. If North does not do so South should pass. It might be that four spades can be defeated or that five diamonds will cost too much. By waiting until the later round South is showing a lack of co-operation that is essential in sacrificial positions.

When either defender has pre-empted, a sacrifice bid should not be made if the hand contains any reasonable prospect of defeating the adverse contract. It is wise to remember that pre-emptive bids put the opposition under pressure and make the accurate interchange of information difficult. They may well have gone too high. The following shows the degree of recklessness that can occur.

South Dealer
North-South Vul.

```
                        North
                        ♠ 4 2
                        ♡ K Q 6 3
                        ◊ J 7 3 2
                        ♣ 7 5 3

West                                              East
♠ Q J 10 9 8 7 6 3                                ♠ 5
♡ -                                               ♡ 10 5 2
◊ 6                                               ◊ Q 9 8 5 4
♣ K 8 6 2                                         ♣ A 10 9 4

                        South
                        ♠ A K
                        ♡ A J 9 8 7 4
                        ◊ A K 10
                        ♣ Q J
```

S	W	N	E
2 H	4 S	5 H	-
6 H	6 S	-	-
6 NT	7 S	Dbl.	-

After South's Acol Two bid showing eight or more playing tricks, West was correct to put up a barrage with four spades to make it difficult for North. When South bid six hearts following the competitive raise to five hearts, he was guessing. It was certainly tempting and he may have been goaded by the thought that West was trying to keep him out. At this point West should have passed, having made his bid on the first round. His partner was equally alive to the need to sacrifice but it was significant that he had not shewn any ability to co-operate by bidding five spades over five hearts.

However, West succeeded in goading South into a further unsound bid of six no trumps. This was probably accountable to the fact that South did not consider that the penalty from doubling six spades would compensate for the loss of a vulnerable slam or game. Actually West does well and might get out for two down in six spades if he guesses the clubs right. But there was no stopping West, self-appointed generalissimo. He was convinced that it was up to him to fight to the bitter end.

Accepting a Penalty

Here again the tactics in match pointed pairs are different from those in teams. In the latter it is generally advisable to ensure a plus score at all costs, even though the penalty may not be as high as was hoped. To collect 500 from a double of five clubs bid sacrificially against your four spades shows a loss of 120 but that is better than going down in five spades, making a swing of 720.

But in pairs it may be no more disastrous to go down than to accept an inadequate penalty. Remember, the paramount need is to get a result as good as at least half the other competitors. If every other pair in your position has scored 620 or 650 you get nought for scoring 500. You also get nought for losing 100.

It is this fact that enables non-vulnerable opponents to take great liberties against vulnerable adversaries. To double at the one level is very dangerous, for if you hold a good hand you can probably make a game and it is difficult to be sure of defeating their contract by four tricks. If you think you can make game you cannot afford to double opponents unless you are convinced the penalty will be worth it. For example, your side is vulnerable

> ♠ K 10 6
> ♡ A Q 2
> ◇ 7
> ♣ A K J 10 8 4
>
> ♠ A 5
> ♡ J 9 5 4
> ◇ K 9 5 2
> ♣ Q 7 6

S	W	N	E
	1 D	3 C	-
3 NT	4 D	-	-
4NT	-	-	-

West was prepared to be doubled in four diamonds, hoping to lose only 500. South could not confidently expect to defeat the diamond contract by four but felt confident of making four no trumps.

The fear that a double may not prove worth while provides some peculiar situations. Suppose West, not vulnerable, opens a weak no trump, doubled by your partner sitting North. East passes and you hold

$$\spadesuit \ \text{K 6 3}$$
$$\heartsuit \ \text{Q 10 7 4}$$
$$\diamondsuit \ \text{A 6 4 2}$$
$$\clubsuit \ \text{J 3}$$

Normally you will pass confidently, expecting to defeat the contract by three or four tricks for 500-700. In a pairs tournament the position is not so simple. Assuming partner holds 15 or 16 points for his double you have the value for game yourself for a score of 600. If there is a slip in defence declarer may well escape for 500 or even 300. It could easily be right to bid three no trumps, a bid you would not normally consider making. On balance it is probably right to pass. For one thing the penalty may well amount to 700. For another, even though you and your partner may have a combined holding of 25 or 26 high card points it may still not be certain that you can make game.

Occasionally you may be completely fixed and a bad result is inevitable, as was the case on this hand from a Swedish tournament.

North Dealer

North — South Vul.

```
                    North
                    ♠ A J 7 6
                    ♡ A K 3
                    ◇ K 9 6 2
                    ♣ J 4
West                                    East
♠ -                                     ♠ 5 3 2
♡ 10 5 2                                ♡ Q 8 6
◇ A 10 7 4                              ◇ Q 8 5
♣ Q 10 8 5 3 2                          ♣ A K 9 7
                    South
                    ♠ K Q 10 9 8 4
                    ♡ J 9 7 4
                    ◇ J 3
                    ♣ 6
```

North opened one spade and South raised to four spades. West bid four no trumps indicating a minor two suited hand and East bid five clubs. A double of five clubs was scarcely likely to produce 700 so South bid five spades and went one down. As the majority of the North — South pairs had been allowed to play in four spades a bad result was unavoidable.

A similar position may arise in a slam. If you bid six hearts vulnerable and non-vulnerable opponents bid six spades as a sacrifice it is extremely unlikely that you will be able to defeat them by eight tricks, necessary to get a penalty of 1500, more than the value of your slam. You may have to consider bidding seven hearts or six no trumps if there is a reasonable chance of success. But if any higher bid by you is unlikely to make, you must double and hope that the penalty is larger than the value of game, in which case you will do better than those who have not reached a slam.

Penalty Doubles

The pitfalls of doubling freely bid games and slams on high cards are well known. Caution is needed at duplicate, particularly in match pointed events. Provided that you do not consider your cards are worth a plus score on their own merit there is seldom any need to double to get a good result. For example, with East — West vulnerable and South dealer the bidding proceeded

S	N
1 S	2 D
2 H	4 S

East held ♠Q J 10 ♡K 10 3 ◇K 5 4 ♣A K 5 3 and passed. The contract went three down and East — West scored 150. This was a top. They would have scored no more points had they doubled. It seemed unlikely that four spades would be made but there might have been a freak distribution. Dummy did hold a singleton club which removed one trick. The point is that the opponents have either bid too boldly or they have not. If they have been over-optimistic you will probably get a good result as other pairs will have stopped in a part score. If they have bid well you may get a fair score by not doubling. Here are two examples from club tournaments.

North Dealer
East — West Vul.

North
♠ K Q 10 9 7 4
♡ Q
◇ K 5
♣ A Q 9 4

West
♠ J 8 6 3
♡ A K 7 6 4
◇ A Q
♣ J 2

East
♠ -
♡ 10 8 5 3
◇ J 7 6 4 2
♣ 8 7 6 3

South
♠ A 5 2
♡ J 9 2
◇ 10 9 8 3
♣ K 10 5

At most tables North — South bid to four spades making eleven tricks (450). This turned out to be below average as many had been doubled. It must have been clear to West that his side were unlikely to be missing anything.

North Dealer
North — South Vul.

North
♠ A K Q 10 6 4 3
♡ Q J
♢ A J 4
♣ J

West
♠ 8 7
♡ A 10 3 2
♢ 3 2
♣ A 10 8 6 2

East
♠ 2
♡ K 9 8 7 5 4
♢ Q 10 7 6
♣ K 4

South
♠ J 9 5
♡ 6
♢ K 9 8 5
♣ Q 9 7 5 3

S	W	N	E
		1 S	2 H
2 S	3 H	4 S	5 H
-	-	5 S	-
-	Dbl:	-	-

South passed East's five hearts bid leaving the decision to North who went five spades. With a seven card suit which had been supported it seemed unlikely that five hearts would cost 700. West made a mistake in doubling. North — South had the balance of strength and East — West were merely pushing. If they had succeeded in pushing their opponents too high they were assured of a good result. If five spades were made they would simply make matters worse by doubling. The contract was made and gained an equal top.

In true competitive situations the position is different. It may be necessary to double in order to gain sufficient points to make up for the loss of a part score. In those cases the incentive is greater if opponents are vulnerable. Often the contract may go one down only for a score of 200, larger than any part score.

Consider the following situation. At game all you open one heart and the next player bids one spade. Your partner raises to two hearts which brings forth two spades from the next player. You bid three hearts which is passed round to your right hand opponent who bids three spades. You hold.

♠ A 5
♡ A K 9 7 6
◇ Q 10 8
♣ Q 10 6

It does not seem likely that you can make four hearts although you expected to make three hearts. You think three spades may go one down but not more. If you were due to score 140 it will not be much use collecting 100 so you should double and try to make 200. Of course you may fail and they will score game as a result of your double. But in practice your match point score will not be so very much worse than it would have been had you passed. If they make three spades they will get a good score as they will have reached the optimum contract. They will have bid to the point beyond which you cannot go without incurring defeat. Should you advance to four hearts they will double and you will lose 200. If you pass and the contract of three spades is made for a score of 140 you will also do badly as other pairs will have been allowed to play in two hearts or three hearts. If three spades goes down and you collect 100 you will do badly but if you double and get 200 you will get a fine result.

When you are satisfied that the opponents' bidding has robbed you of a part score, a penalty double is indicated, always provided that it is unsafe for you to bid any higher yourself and that there is a reasonable chance of defeating them. It is no use doubling recklessly but it is often clear, particularly after an opening one no trump, that you hold the balance of strength and that a double will succeed.

North Dealer
Game All

                        North
                        ♠ A J 4
                        ♡ K 9 6 2
                        ◇ 7 6
                        ♣ A 8 5 4

West   East   East
♠ K 9 8 3 2   ♠ 6 5
♡ 10 4 3   ♡ Q 7 5
◇ K 9 8   ◇ A Q 5 4
♣ 10 3   ♣ K Q 9 2

                        South
                        ♠ Q 10 7
                        ♡ A J 8
                        ◇ J 10 3 2
                        ♣ J 7 6

S	W	N	E
		1 NT	Dbl.
		(12-14)	
-	2 S	-	-
Dbl.			

Result — West went two down and lost 500. East should not have doubled with only 13 points and West should have passed with 6 points. Maybe he was accustomed to his partner doubling weak no trumps below strength. South appreciated that his side held the balance of strength with at least 21 points against 19. Even a one trick defeat would be worth 200 with only a part score at most available.

A further example:
West Dealer
Love All

```
                      North
                      ♠ A J
                      ♡ K J 7 4
                      ◇ Q 8 3 2
                      ♣ K J 5
West                                   East
♠ Q 10 9 6 2                           ♠ 4 3
♡ A Q 3                                ♡ 10 9 6 2
◇ 6 4                                  ◇ A K 10 5
♣ A 8 7                                ♣ Q 10 6
                      South
                      ♠ K 8 7 5
                      ♡ 8 5
                      ◇ J 9 7
                      ♣ 9 4 3 2
```

S	W	N	E
	1 S	Dbl.	Redbl.
1 NT	Dbl.	-	-

West knows that his partner holds at least 9 points so that his side has the balance of strength; the double resulted in a penalty of 500. Even if South passes over the redouble, leaving it to his partner to take it out, his side are bound to concede a fair-sized penalty.

Weak and Strong No Trump

The supporters of the weak no trump can claim the following advantages:

1. The pre-emptive value of the bid may enable the partnership to make a part score where a lower opening would have allowed the opponents to compete.
2. On grounds of frequency there are more hands ranging between 12-14 points than between 16-18 or 15-17.
3. The part score, being in no trumps, may produce a higher score than in a suit. This is by no means always the case.
4. The fact that the partner of the opener may pass one no trump with

as much as 10 or even 11 points can create a difficult problem for the fourth player who may hold a fair hand and is tempted to compete. At match points you cannot neglect the chance of fighting for a part score. With ten points in responder's hand any intervention can be profitably doubled.

5. The knowledge that the opener's hand is limited to a maximum of 14 points often permits the deal to be played in the only makeable contract. For example, opener bids one no trump and partner with ten points passes, giving a combined count of 24, not usually enough for game. It sometimes happens that the cards lie perversely and only seven tricks can be made. In this event you are likely to get a good score as other pairs may find it difficult to stop below two no trumps.

The chief drawbacks are:

1. The bid can on occasions result in a large adverse penalty. This is not such a disaster as it might appear. If you lose 1100 or 1400 you get a bottom, but you cannot lose the tournament on one board. If you make one less trick than everyone else in a contract of say two spades you also get a bottom.

2. You may miss a part score in a major suit, e.g. you may open one no trump on

$$
\begin{array}{l}
\spadesuit \ \text{K J 7 5} \\
\heartsuit \ \text{K 8 3} \\
\diamondsuit \ \text{A Q 8 4} \\
\clubsuit \ \text{J 6}
\end{array}
$$

If left in you may find partner with four spades which probably means you could have done better in a suit. This seems to be a major disadvantage. Often players open one no trump and scramble seven tricks but could have made two in a major suit for 110. A further disadvantage is the difficulty in contesting the bidding after one no trump is overcalled with a suit. In the above example, suppose the next player overcalls with two hearts and your partner holds about eight points including four spades headed by the queen. It is hard to suggest any suitable bid he can make and you cannot do more. So you have lost the initiative; had you opened with one spade, partner could support to two spades.

3. The introduction of modern defensive measures has taken away much of the effectiveness of the weak no trump. The advantages included the pre-emptive nature of the bid which resulted in

opponents being robbed of a part score. But these are lessened by using one of the standard defences, such as Sharples, Astro, Landy, Cansino and Ripstra.

Many players play weak throughout, i.e. whether vulnerable or not. The chief drawback to this is the loss of 200 by going two down vulnerable, not doubled. The occasional loss of 1100 or 1400 is less important. It is a bottom but the loss can be recovered on the next board.

Some players prefer what is called the 'three quarter no trump'. This means that they play the weak no trump at all times except when they are vulnerable and the other side are not. There does not appear to be any advantage in this. Besides the effort required in noticing the score and avoiding a misunderstanding by forgetting what you have arranged, a no trump that crashes is probably a bottom anyway.

If you go two down vulnerable, undoubled, and lose 200 it really does not matter whether the opponents are vulnerable or not. The same applies to a penalty of 800. Only if the loss is kept to 500 will the vulnerability of the opponents be material. If they are game and can make 3 no trumps your loss of 500 is cheap compared with the 600 they might have scored, whereas it would be expensive if the other side were not vulnerable and would only have scored 400. But this is a rare situation. If oponents can make game you are almost certainly going at least three down, which is 800 if vulnerable. If you are only two down (-500) it is unlikely the other side have a game. In this case your loss is a disaster.

In order to obtain the best results from the weak no trump the following points should be borne in mind.

It is better to avoid making a weakness take-out on a poor hand unless the contract is doubled or your suit is spades. Thus pass an opening bid of one no trump vulnerable on:

(a)   ♠ 5 3
         ♡ Q 10 7 6 2
         ◊ A 3 2
         ♣ J 7 5

(b) ♠ 7 4
  ♡ J 4 3
  ◇ J 8 6 3 2
  ♣ Q 4 2

(c) ♠ Q 7 6
  ♡ K Q 8 4 3
  ◇ Q 5 4
  ♣ 10 6

The result of a take-out into two hearts or two diamonds will be to enable the opponents to come in, probably with spades. If both partners have announced moderate hands the task of the defenders is made easier, and the risks in contesting the auction much reduced. But if you pass there is always the possibility that you hold up to 9 or 10 points and opponents may not risk competing.

On hand (b) it is unlikely that you will be left unmolested and if the no trump bid is doubled a retreat to two diamonds must be made. But there is always the possibility that the adverse strength is divided in which case neither can double and you should get a good result. Vulnerable a take-out must certainly be made on hand (b) as you cannot afford to go down at the rate of 100 per trick. Hands (a) and (c) are sufficiently good to make a rescue unnecessary.

With a five card spade suit the position is different and the pre-emptive value of two spades assists in silencing the opponents. Thus respond two spades on

    ♠ A J 9 6 5
    ♡ 4 3
    ◇ Q 10 8 6
    ♣ 10 2

Redouble of No Trump

If your partner's one no trump is doubled on your right many players redouble holding ten points. It is true that it may lead to a profitable double of the opponents when they take it out. But it does not always work out as hoped, as witness the occasion in the final of the Middlesex County Pairs when the bidding went

S	W	N	E
1 NT	Dbl.	Redbl.	-
-	-		

West had a solid suit and the contract went three down! In fact there is really no necessity to redouble. If all pass the contract is likely to be made with an overtrick. Even if just made, 180 for one no trump doubled and made is seldom a bad result. The only time you might lose is if you make two overtricks, and score 380 not vulnerable. This is 20 points less than the value of game you appear to have been able to make. But, assuming the double is based on 15-16 points it is far from certain that game will be both bid and made at other tables.

If you pass and the next player takes out the double you still have all your options open to double for penalties. There is much to be said for the SOS Redouble. If the opener's partner redoubles following a second hand double, e.g.

S	W	N	E
1 NT	Dbl.	Redbl.	-

this implies a very bad hand unwilling to play in one no trump doubled. The opener should rescue into his lowest four card suit and aim at finding a better spot in a suit. Opponents often fail to make the best of their superior forces in these circumstances. A further advantage is the negative inference available to the opener. A pass by his partner implies that he has a few points and that there is a sporting chance of making the contract. Suppose declarer has opened one no trump on:

♠ 9 5 2
♡ K 4
♢ A Q 8 6 4
♣ K 10 2

and is doubled on his left. Using standard methods, if the next two players pass he has to decide whether to stick it out or retreat to two diamonds. To run out into two diamonds would be a mistake if partner held 8 or 9 points. Using the SOS Redouble the position is clearer. If partner passes, you pass as there must be a chance.

Mini No Trump

During the past few years a super weak no trump on 10-12 points has become popular in England. It was originated by British international Alan Hiron; the mechanics are briefly as follows. The basic principle is that you never play in one no trump doubled. You may be doubled in a suit or you may play one no trump redoubled.

1. Opening bid = 10-12 points balanced.
2. Responder requires 13 (possibly good 12) to raise to two no trumps, and 14 or more to bid three no trumps, or force in a suit.
3. Responder takes out on a poor hand with 5 cards or longer suit.
4. If doubled second in hand, responder rescues into a five card suit with a poor hand, otherwise passes.
5. Opener must redouble. This is automatic. If partner has a fair hand — 9 or 10 points or over — he passes and if left in game will be made. If partner is weak he bids his lowest four card suit and rescue operations begin in search of a 4-3 fit or better. Partner should avoid bidding two spades as this is uneconomical.
6. If one no trump is doubled on opener's right, i.e. by fourth hand, opener redoubles and the drill is the same as in 5 above. As partner did not take out into a suit on the first round, the inference is that he does not hold a five card suit.

This is a tactical bid and the automatic redouble puts great pressure on opponents, especially if passed out. Defending one no trump redoubled is nerve-racking as the consequences resulting from a defensive slip are disastrous.

The mini no trump should only be used in first or second position non-vulnerable. After partner has passed there is no point as you are probably out-gunned.

The chief disadvantage occurs when you are doubled with 10 points facing 7. You are likely to lose 300 in your suit rescue and with 23 points combined there is unlikely to be a biddable game for the other side. In theory this is no worse than having 12 opposite to 5 in a weak no trump, when the result may also be much the same. But with the mini no trump you are likely to be out on your own as other pairs may not have opened.

Another awkward situation is when you hold 12 points and partner holds 12 and passes. With the cards lying well you make nine tricks. Standard weak no trump bidders will probably reach game by the simple route one no trump — three no trumps.

There are snags to all methods, but the mini no trump produces some fine results and plenty of excitement!

8

PAIRS CONTESTS : TACTICS IN PLAY
THE PERSONAL FACTOR

In all pairs events it is important to remember that you are competing against several other couples. If you bid and play naturally you are likely to find other competitors with a similar result to your own. Whether it is good or bad. Some players seek to achieve results entirely different from anyone else. They indulge in frequent bluff bids and take hideous risks to try and make overtricks. Such tactics are basically unsound and unlikely to result in consistent success. Suppose, for example, you decide to go all out bidding games and slams on the slightest pretext. You start off by reaching three no trumps on a combined count of 22 points with no long suit. With a lucky distribution and helped by faulty defence you make the contract and score a top. A few boards later you embark on a similar exploit and again bid three no trumps with 23 points between you. This time you are less lucky and go two down. As no-one else has reached game you get a bottom and you have achieved exactly average on the two boards. Certainly no more than you would have achieved had you played normal bridge.

It is only too easy to remember the tops you get through bidding and making games and slams you should not be in. But one is apt to forget the bottoms through such tactics. In point of fact you will find on careful analysis of your results that the tops and bottoms cancel each other out.

Shooting for tops and bottoms so that your score if recorded in the shape of a graph would look like a scenic railway can never be recommended. The only possible excuse for such tactics would be in the case of a pair who felt completely outclassed and held no chance but for a consistent run of good luck.

Shooting to recover a bad board is also not to be recommended. Many players, having scored a zero on one board will seek to get it back on the next. In most cases the result is merely another zero. Match pointed competitions cannot be won or lost on one board alone. If you have a disaster and go down 1400 you will almost certainly get a bottom. Later you may succeed in making a modest contract of two clubs for a top. You are now average on the two boards. Match points can be regained by steady play so long as you have a little luck in the shape of opponents' mistakes. To indulge in reckless bidding just because you have no chance is wrong and apt to spoil the contest. It is also unfair to other players.

Suppose you start off against Mr and Mrs A, a fairly strong pair, and make out a little below average on your two boards. After leaving your table things start going wrong for Mr and Mrs A and they begin to fight and bicker. By the time it comes to the last round they are so disinterested in the whole thing that they probably present two tops to your nearest rivals, who as a result beat you by a small margin. You are unlucky in that you played against this pair before they became demoralized.

The folly of underestimating your adversaries has already been stressed. This common error is the cause of many surprise results in important events. This is what frequently occurs. A final is made up of, say, nine expert and five weak pairs. The experts form the view that they cannot expect many gifts from each other and therefore they must go for tops against the rabbits. In stretching for the impossible they end up by giving tops instead of receiving them and some unknown pair duly wins.

If in doubt try and play as you think others in your position will do. If you are undecided whether to bid one more for game, pass. If the game is on it is presumably difficult to bid and there will surely be others who have not reached it, even though it is unbeatable.

If you have an awkward choice of leads, play with the room. For example, the bidding has gone

S	N
1 D	1 S
2 D	3 NT

You are East holding:

♠ K 10 8 4 2   ♡ Q 3   ◇ J 7 4 2   ♣ Q 3

Yours is not an easy lead. A diamond cannot be good and spades have been bid on your right. However, you should not risk a desperation lead from one of your queens for this might prove too costly if it went wrong. It is better to lead a spade. For one thing North's bid may be a bluff to inhibit the lead or it may be based on a shaded suit, such as A x x x or J x x x. Partner may still hold a spade honour. Also it is possible that at other tables the bidding has been

1 D   3 NT

in which case a spade is the probable lead. Even if it turns out badly you will be in company.

A similar principle is involved with a two way finesse. You are declarer in a spade contract and the trump suit is

K 9 8 4

A J 10 5

There has been no adverse bidding and there are no clues at all regarding the position of the queen. Nor is there any reason to keep out one defender rather than the other. Playing against weak opponents you can lead ♠J, expecting it to be covered, and, if not, play ♠K and finesse towards your hand. But assuming the defenders to be of reasonable standard and ♠J would not be covered anyway, you are probably "with the room" to run the knave. Many players play "queen over knave", a theory based on the principle (probably fallacious) that the queen will probably have taken the knave in the previous deal and an imperfect shuffle has left these two cards together. Be that as it may, with nothing else to guide you, you will be following the crowd and should get some points even if you go down.

Conversely, if you are not doing well and need points badly it will pay you to finesse in the opposite direction in the hope that you are right and all the others wrong.

Knowledge of the style of bidding and play of other contestants in your line may influence your decisions. For example, assume you are East – West in your local club's weekly duplicate. You will most probably have acquired a fair knowledge of the players and their capabilities. If you see several other East – West pairs whom you know to be forward bidders, you can be bold yourself.

Tactics in Play

Pairs tournaments governed by match points demand a special technique in regard to the play. This is the result of the peculiar conditions whereby it is essential to record a better score on each board than your rivals. Whether the score is better or worse by 10 or 1000 is immaterial. Your triumph or disaster is confined to that particular board. One of the first things to appreciate is the vital importance of overtricks. Making the contract is not enough in itself. If not vulnerable you make four spades scoring 420 when everyone else has made eleven tricks and scored 450, you will get nought just as if you had gone down.

The importance of the overtrick is just as great in a part score as in a game or slam. Take this example from the World Olympic Mixed Pairs in Amsterdam 1966.

South Dealer
East — West Vul.

```
                          North
                          ♠ 5 4
                          ♡ A 7 5 2
                          ◇ J 10 8 3 2
                          ♣ 7 4
     West                                      East
     ♠ J 10 7 6                                ♠ 9 3
     ♡ Q 10 6 4                                ♡ K 9 3
     ◇ 9 7                                     ◇ K Q 6 4
     ♣ Q 10 5                                  ♣ K 9 8 2
                          South
                          ♠ A K Q 8 2
                          ♡ J 8
                          ◇ A 5
                          ♣ A J 6 3
```

S	W	N	E
1 S	-	-	Dbl.
2 C	2 H	-	-
2 S	-	-	-

Those who made eight tricks, scoring 110, obtained an above average result, but A. Hjertstrand and Mrs Werner of Sweden who finished 15th out of 130 pairs did even better by making an overtrick.

West led ♡ 4 won in dummy and a club was ducked to West who returned a low heart. East won with ♡ K and led back a trump. South

won with ♠A, cashed ♣A and ruffed ♣3 in dummy. He entered his hand
with a heart ruff and played off♠K Q before putting West on lead with
the last trump, leaving this position

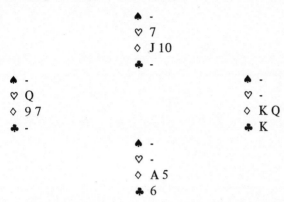

```
                          ♠ -
                          ♡ 7
                          ◇ J 10
                          ♣ -
       ♠ -                                   ♠ -
       ♡ Q                                   ♡ -
       ◇ 9 7                                 ◇ K Q
       ♣ -                                   ♣ K
                          ♠ -
                          ♡ -
                          ◇ A 5
                          ♣ 6
```

West was well pleased to be on lead with the master heart and no more
trumps left in the game. He cashed ♡ Q and in doing so squeezed his
partner who was unable to retain a guard in diamonds and protect the
clubs.

An overtrick resulting from a pointless third in hand bid made a big
difference on this hand from the Ladies Pairs Championship at
Amsterdam.

West-Dealer
North — South Vul.

```
                       North
                       ♠ Q J
                       ♡ A 8 7 2
                       ◇ K 10 8
                       ♣ 10 9 6 2
West                                        East
♠ 9 8 7                                     ♠ K 6 5 4 2
♡ 5 3                                       ♡ K J 6
◇ J 6 5 4 2                                 ◇ 9 7 3
♣ A 5 4                                     ♣ Q 8
                       South
                       ♠ A 10 3
                       ♡ Q 10 9 4
                       ◇ A Q
                       ♣ K J 7 3
```

S	W	N	E
	-	-	1 S
1 NT	-	2 S	-
3 H	-	4 H	-

North's bid of two spades was designed to find out if partner held the other major. West led ♠9 and ♠J held the trick. Normally it would be correct play to lead trumps twice from the South hand, playing for divided honours, but armed with the information supplied by East's bid, South played ♡A and ♡2. East won and tried a deceptive return of ♣8 but declarer needed the club finesse in any event so let it run to West's ♣A. The club return was taken with ♣K and the remaining trumps drawn and eleven tricks made.

East's third in hand bid was pointless as it had no lead directing value and merely assisted declarer to play the hand. Scoring an overtrick was worth 30 match points out of 42 to Mrs J Gruver and Mrs D. Sachs of U.S.A. who finished runners up to the British pair, Mrs J. Durran and Mrs J. Juan (now Mrs Priday). Those who only made ten tricks in hearts only scored 10 match points as several pairs bid and made an overtrick in no trumps.

This aspect of the game is open to the very reasonable criticism that it is possible to gain a top by bad play, just as it is possible that, by displaying faultless technique, you may be rewarded by getting a bottom. Here is a simple example:

> ♠ K 5 3
> ♡ K J 6
> ◇ A Q 10 9 4
> ♣ 5 2
>
> ♠ A 9 8
> ♡ A Q 3 2
> ◇ J 8 6
> ♣ A 8 7

You are South in three No Trumps. West leads ♣6, East playing ♣Q. Playing rubber bridge or in teams you hold up your ace until the third round. This makes the contract a virtual certainty, even though the diamond finesse is wrong. Either East will not have a club to return or the suit is divided 4-4.

Playing match points the position is not so straightforward. If ◊K is with West you can make twelve tricks, but if you play safe you will make only eleven. If you gamble and do not hold up you may well go down. On the other hand you may get a bottom for making only eleven tricks if everyone else has taken a chance and made twelve, or possibly received a different opening lead, giving time to risk the diamond finesse.

Advice in such cases is difficult to give, but the best course is to duck the first round and see what is returned. You can afford to do this as here is no real hope of making all thirteen tricks. Should East return ♣3, take it. It looks as though the clubs will be divided 4-4 in which case you will not go down. Equally if, as you assume, East has four clubs, holding up will not help. If ♣3 is not East's fourth best, it is probable that West started with a six card suit and one hold up is enough. But in this event West's suit would be ♣K J 10 9 6 4 and the normal lead would have been ♣J, or possibly ♣K in an endeavour to pin a singleton queen.

If East returns ♣9 at trick two it is better to hold up to the third round as there is a big danger of West holding five. You then hope for the diamond finesse to be wrong so that your correct technique may meet with its just reward.

Safety Plays

The necessity for making every possible trick raises a big problem in considering the advisability of making a safety play. It may be convenient to consider this matter under two headings: those safety plays which do not involve the sacrifice of a trick and those that do.

A. Safety Plays that do not Sacrifice a Trick

These types of plays are mainly designed to guard against a bad division of trumps or a bad distribution of an outside suit. They may be referred to as Safety Situations.

This hand from a club tournament illustrates the need to make an unblocking safety play to make overtricks.

South Dealer
Love All

```
                      North
                      ♠ Q J 8 5
                      ♥ 4 2
                      ◊ A Q 9 8 3
                      ♣ K Q
West                                      East
♠ K 3                                     ♠ A 7 4 2
♥ Q J 10 9 8                              ♥ K 7 5 3
◊ J 6 5 2                                 ◊ 7
♣ 6 3                                     ♣ 10 8 5 2
                      South
                      ♠ 10 9 6
                      ♥ A 6
                      ◊ K 10 4
                      ♣ A J 9 7 4
```

S	W	N	E
1 NT	-	2 C	-
2 D	-	3 NT	

North responded two clubs to investigate a possible game in spades, but South denied a four card major suit. West led ♥Q taken with ♥A. There are nine top tricks with 5 clubs, 3 diamonds and 1 heart, but there is a good chance of making all the diamonds. After cashing dummy's ♣K and Q, ◊A is played, South unblocking with ◊10. Next ◊3 is led and the position revealed when East discards a heart. South wins with ◊K and plays off his three clubs and returns ◊4, finessing dummy's ◊9.

This gives him 5 diamonds, 5 clubs and 1 heart for eleven tricks. Had he not played ◊10 on ◊A the suit would be blocked, for when ◊10 was led West would not cover and South could not afford to overtake with ◊Q.

Here is a further example from a County Pairs tournament.

North Dealer

Game All

```
                          North
                          ♠ A Q
                          ♡ 9 7 6
                          ◇ Q J 10 3 2
                          ♣ A 10 6
West                                              East
♠ 10 8 6 5 3                                      ♠ 9 7 4 2
♡ J 10 8 3                                        ♡ A 5 4
◇ K 8 5                                           ◇ A 7
♣ 3                                               ♣ J 7 5 2
                          South
                          ♠ K J
                          ♡ K Q 2
                          ◇ 9 6 4
                          ♣ K Q 9 8 4
```

South is declarer in three no trumps and West leads ♠5, taken in dummy with ♠Q, East signalling with ♠7. There is no time to establish diamonds and the only hope is to make two tricks in hearts in addition to 5 clubs and 2 spades. At trick two a low heart is led and East ducks. South wins with ♡K. South next plays ♣K and is careful to unblock ♣10 from the table. He continues with a low club to the ace, the distribution being revealed when West discards ◇8. Another low heart from dummy is ducked by East and won with ♡K. Dummy is re-entered with ♠A and ♣6 led and the marked finesse taken against ♣J. It would not have helped East to win earlier with ♡A as ♡Q would be an entry to the closed hand. But it was vital to unblock ♣10, otherwise South would not get back without overtaking with ♣Q and later losing to ♣J.

These two hands illustrate safety play in dealing with a card combination.

The next hand can be classified as a safety play in that it seeks to guard against unnecessary defeat. It cannot guarantee the contract but is designed to provide an additional chance.

South Dealer
Love All

North
♠ 6 4
♡ K Q 5
◊ 9 8 6 5 4
♣ 10 3 2

West
♠ Q J 10 7 3
♡ J 9 8
◊ K
♣ 8 6 5 4

East
♠ K 8 2
♡ 10 4 3 2
◊ J 7 3
♣ Q J 7

South
♠ A 9 5
♡ A 7 6
◊ A Q 10 2
♣ A K 9

South opens two no trumps and is raised to three no trumps. West leads ♠Q to which East follows with ♠8 and South ducks. West continues with ♠7 and East's ♠K is allowed to hold. South wins the third round. Clearly West must be kept out of the lead and if he holds the guarded king of diamonds this will not be possible. If ◊K is with East it will not matter as he is unlikely to have a spade to return. If he has, the suit is divided 4-4. The only situation where West could gain the lead when it might have been prevented is if he has a singleton king.

Therefore South crosses to dummy with ♡Q and leads a diamond. When East plays low South plays ◊A. It is lucky that ◊K falls, but if it had not, South would have returned to dummy and led another. If East had the king it would not matter.

It would be wrong for declarer to play ◊A from hand. East might hold the singleton ◊K in which case West with ◊J x x would have an entry. By playing the diamonds from dummy, South can duck if ◊K comes up from East.

A further example of a safety play designed to give an extra chance occurred in the London Masters Individual Championship.

South Dealer
East — West Vul.

                        North
                        ♠ Q 6 4
                        ♡ Q J 8 7
                        ◊ J 7
                        ♣ Q 9 6 4
West   East
♠ J 10 9 5 3 2   ♠ K 8 7
♡ 4   ♡ 6 2
◊ 3   ◊ Q 10 9 4 2
♣ A K J 10 7   ♣ 8 5 2
                        South
                        ♠ A
                        ♡ A K 10 9 5 3
                        ◊ A K 8 6 5
                        ♣ 3

After a game forcing opening bid of two clubs and a spade overcall from West, South became declarer in six hearts. West led ♣A and switched to ♠J. The contract appears to be a lay-down and it is in such cases that the need for extra care is so important. The only possible danger is a bad distribution of diamonds. If they are 3-3 or 4-2 it is simple. But if they are 5-1 it will require three trumps in dummy to ruff three times. To provide for this chance only one round of trumps is played, followed by ◊A K. If all follow there is no problem. As it is, West fails but had no trump card. "How lucky can you be" may be your re-action to this, but it is a perfectly logical play. If West had ruffed you are down. You could have prevented this by drawing his trump, but you would have lost a trick in diamonds instead.

A similar situation arose recently in a club duplicate pairs event.

North Dealer
Game All

              North
              ♠ K 3 2
              ♡ 7 6 3
              ◊ A K 9 5
              ♣ A K 4

West   East
♠ 9 8 5   ♠ 10 6
♡ J 10 8 2   ♡ 4
◊ 7   ◊ Q J 10 8 6 3 2
♣ Q 7 5 3 2   ♣ J 10 8

              South
              ♠ A Q J 7 4
              ♡ A K Q 9 5
              ◊ 4
              ♣ 9 6

S	W	N	E
		1 NT	-
3 S	-	4 S	-
4 NT	-	5 H	-
5 NT	-	6 S	-
7 S			

West led a trump, won with ♠J. Again, the contract looks to be straightforward. The only danger is that the hearts do not break. South drew a second round of trumps with ♠K and played two rounds of hearts. Had both opponents followed he could draw the last trump and claim the rest. As it was, when East showed out it was necessary to play a third top heart and ruff one in dummy. After cashing ◊A, the closed hand was entered by ruffing a diamond with ♠Q. The last trump was drawn with ♠A and the fifth heart along with ♣A and K making the contract.

The majority only reached six spades or six no trumps making twelve tricks. One pair bid and made seven spades and one pair bid seven no trumps and went down. This is a further illustration of the point that it is quite unnecessary to risk playing in no trumps to try and gain 10 more points. If you bid a grand slam and make it you will seldom, if ever, get a bad result.

B. Safety Plays that involve the possible Sacrifice of a Trick

This is a more difficult problem. With match point scoring you cannot really afford to give away any unnecessary tricks, for making fewer tricks than others may result in the same disastrous result as going down. When one refers to unnecessary tricks, this relates to tricks which might not have been conceded if a bolder policy in play had been adopted. No trick can be considered unnecessary if it means the difference between making and losing the contract. But in deciding the degree of caution needed you must weigh up the frequency of the contingency against which you are protecting yourself.

Earlier in this book this example of safety play was given in discussing tactics in teams.

♠ 7
♡ 8 6 3
◊ 5 4
♣ A K J 7 5 4 3

♠ A Q 2
♡ A 10 5 4
◊ A J 9 3
♣ 6 2

South is in three no trumps. West leads a spade. In order to make certain of the contract you win the first trick and lead a club, playing low from dummy if West follows suit. If all the missing clubs are with East there is nothing you can do. But this play ensures the contract even if West holds ♣Q 10 9 8. Playing in teams there is no argument that this must be the correct play, although it might involve giving up an unnecessary trick if West happened to hold ♣ Q x or ♣ Q x x or even ♣ x x x if you played ♣ A on the first round.

Playing pairs you have to decide between three possible plays:

(1) Playing off ♣ A K and hoping for the drop of ♣ Q
(2) Finessing ♣ J
(3) Ducking completely

Alternative (1) is unsound as there is a fair probability that ♣Q will not fall, in which case the suit is completely wasted. The gamble might be considered if your position were desperate and you were prepared to risk a complete zero in order to gain a possible top. The second alternative is more reasonable. It combines a reasonable chance of making all seven clubs, whilst at the same time involving a small risk of defeat if the clubs divide 4-0, which represents a 10% chance. If all the clubs are on the right it makes no difference, so that you are risking a 4-0 split on the left, which is 5% (half of 10%).

The third alternative is probably over cautious as it is catering for a situation which will only occur 5% of the time. Again, if you were doing badly and needed a top to put you in contention you might adopt this ultra cautious play in the hope of doing better than those who have been less careful. Other factors that may influence your decision may involve.

Appraising the Contract
(a)   Is the contract likely to be general?
(b)   Have you received a more favourable lead than others may have done.

In the example above it is true that you have only 23 combined high card points and therefore some pairs may not reach three no trumps. Some may play in clubs. But if the bidding starts 1 H − 2 C − 2 NT, the majority of reasonable players will raise to three NT. Similarly, if South opens one NT (15-17) most North players would bid three NT. So, if playing in a reasonable standard game it would be likely that three NT would be a popular contract.

But consider this example
Dealer West
Game All

```
              ♠ J
              ♡ 8 5 3
              ♦ A K Q 5 4 2
              ♣ 9 7 6

              ♠ A K 2
              ♡ A 9 7 6
              ♦ 6 3
              ♣ J 10 8 5
```

S	W	N	E
	1 S	2 D	-
2 NT	-	3 NT	

North raised to game hoping that his hand would provide six winners in diamonds. West led ♠6 and ♠J held the trick. South can see that he can make game even if he makes only five tricks in diamonds. He can therefore afford to duck the first round of diamonds to guard against one opponent holding four.

It looks as though bidding and making game in no trumps will be a good result. There are only 22 combined high card points and there was an opening bid to contend with. In addition the opening lead was favourable, allowing the singleton ♠J to win. If hearts had been attacked it would be necessary to rely on the diamonds breaking 3-2. Nor would the situation be materially altered had the contract been doubled. Defeat by one trick only, losing 200, would be a bad result as your contract is unlikely to be general and your high card strength is sufficient to prevent an adverse game. If the diamonds are 4-1 those in three diamonds will probably also be one down but they may not be doubled and will only lose 100.

Consider this hand from a Congress pairs final.

South Dealer
Game All

```
                    North
                    ♠ 9 7 5
                    ♡ A Q 10 8 4 3
                    ◊ K 2
                    ♣ A 8

West                                    East
♠ Q 8 2                                 ♠ A K 10 3
♡ J 5 2                                 ♡ K
◊ 9 6 5                                 ◊ J 10 7 3
♣ J 10 9 7                              ♣ 5 4 3 2

                    South
                    ♠ J 6 4
                    ♡ 9 7 6
                    ◊ A Q 8 4
                    ♣ K Q 6
```

S	W	N	E
1 NT	-	2 D	-
2 H	-	4 H	-
-	-		

South opened with a weak no trump (12-14 points) and North made a Jacoby Transfer bid of two diamonds requesting partner to convert to the next higher suit (two hearts). This convention is designed to allow the stronger hand to remain concealed. In the case of the weak no trump there may still be slender values that are best protected. North duly raised to game and West made his natural lead of ♣ J.

South won in dummy and laid down ♡ A, being rewarded when ♡ K fell. He entered his hand with ♣ Q, took the marked trump finesse and discarded two of dummy's spades on ♣ K and ◊ A, finishing up with twelve tricks for a top.

Playing ♡ A was a safety play to guard against the loss of two tricks unless ♡ K J x are offside. It is a safety play that may involve the loss of a trick if West happened to hold a doubleton king. But South was tactically correct in his play:

The transfer bid resulted in the hand being played by the short heart hand. With North as declarer it would be likely that East would lead a spade, giving the defence three tricks as a start.

In appraising the contract you have to consider whether the contract is good or bad and whether the result will be above average if you go down.

```
        South Dealer
        North — South Vul.
                            ♠ J 10
                            ♡ A 7 2
                            ◊ K 9 7 3
                            ♣ 7 4 3 2

                            ♠ Q 8
                            ♡ K 9 6
                            ◊ A 6 5
                            ♣ A Q 10 9 5
```

S	W	N	E
1 C	1 S	2 C	-
-	-		

West leads off with ♠A and K, followed by a low heart. Looking at the two hands it appears that you have done well to buy the contract. The other side can almost certainly make two spades and only go one down if ♣K is guarded with East, in which case they will lose two tricks in each side suit. You win the third trick in dummy with ♥ A and lead a low club. Unless East plays an honour, play ♣ A as the standard safety play. If you make 90 for two clubs this will be better than 50 for defeating East – West by one trick not vulnerable in two spades.

As we saw earlier, a favourable lead due to the contract being played from a different side than at other tables may also influence the play.

South Dealer

North – South Vul.

North
♠ A 5
♥ K 4 3
◊ Q 9 8 6 2
♣ K 8 6

West
♠ J 6 3
♥ J 10 9 5
◊ A 5
♣ Q J 3 2

East
♠ K Q 9 7 4 2
♥ 7 6 2
◊ J 10 7 3
♣ -

South
♠ 10 8
♥ A Q 8
◊ K 4
♣ A 10 9 7 5 4

South opened one no trump (12-14 points) and North bid three no trumps. West led ♥ J. South won in hand with ♥ Q and led ♣ 4 and played ♣ 8 when West followed with ♣ 2. Game was duly made with 5 clubs, 3 hearts and 1 spade, opponents switching to spades when in with ♣ Q.

The play of ♣ 8 was a safety play to guard against one opponent holding all four clubs. Had East won the trick with ♣ J or ♣ Q there would only be two clubs outstanding and these would fall on ♣ A and ♣ K. This type of play is a luxury in so far as it may easily give up a trick if the suit is split 2-2, or an honour falls on the first lead enabling a finesse to be taken against the remaining honour. But declarer's play in this instance was justified because the opening lead left him with all suits under control and also because:

(a) the opponents held nine spades between them and other declarers would surely get a spade lead, and

(b)the length in spades is probably with East, who would have had
     the lead in the more likely event of North playing the hand.
   Owing to South's somewhat unorthodox no trump opening, it is
quite likely that at other tables the bidding might have been

	South	1 C	North	2 NT	or
		3 NT			
		1 C		1 D	
		2 C		2 NT	
		3 NT			

In the latter case East might well have intervened with a spade bid and
altered the course of events.
   If you are in a poor contract you cannot afford to make a safety play
to curtail your loss. Going more tricks down will not make much
difference. Such was the case on this hand from the World Olympiad
Mixed Pairs in Amsterdam 1966.

East Dealer
East — West Vul.

                          North
                          ♠ A 10 5
                          ♡ 10 8 5 4
                          ◇ 9 8 7 5
                          ♣ K 10

West   East
♠ Q J   ♠ 9 7 6
♡ Q 7 2   ♡ J 3
◇ A K J 6   ◇ 10 4 2
♣ Q 8 6 5   ♣ J 9 4 3 2

                          South
                          ♠ K 8 4 3 2
                          ♡ A K 9 6
                          ◇ Q 3
                          ♣ A 7

   With Mrs M. Whitaker and C. Goldstein from England sitting
North — South against G. Garabello and Mrs L. Fubini of Italy, the
bidding proceeded

S	W	N	E
			-
1 S	-	2 S	-
3 C	-	4 S	

After the single raise the rebid of three clubs is a trial bid suggesting that game in spades may be made if North's raise is a fair one including values in clubs. Hoping that the doubleton king would be sufficient North bid four spades. West led ◊A and switched to ♠J, taken with dummy's ♠A. In order to protect against a singleton ♠J with West, in which case playing off ♠K would mean losing two tricks if East held ♠ Q 9 7 6, declarer entered his hand with ♡K, led a low trump to ♠10 in dummy. West won with ♠Q and the contract was one down, losing one spade, one heart and two diamonds.

The safety play to avoid a two trick set was wrong. It does not appear from a glance at the hands that many will be in game. Therefore every effort must be made to succeed in the contract and trust that the ♠Q J are bare – the only possible chance. A bold policy would have netted 110 match points. As it was, going one down earned only 5.

Bidding and making a slam seldom scores below average so it is reasonable to employ safety play to ensure the contract, even if the slam is likely to be called at every table owing to the high point count, as in this example

> ♠ A K J
> ♡ A 9 5 4
> ◊ A Q 7
> ♣ A Q 4
>
> ♠ 7 6 5
> ♡ K J 6 2
> ◊ K 6 5
> ♣ K J 3

West leads ◊J against six no trumps. South has only ten top tricks despite his 35 combined points. If the spade finesse succeeds, he is home if he can be sure of three heart tricks. If the spade finesse loses, he will require all four heart tricks, needing a different handling of the suit.

In order to ascertain how many hearts are needed South wins the opening lead in hand and immediately finesses ♠J. If this holds, he

makes a safety play in hearts to ensure three tricks. He leads ♡ 4 to ♡ K
and returns ♡ 2. If West follows low ♡ 9 is played from North. This
guards against one opponent holding Q 10 x x. Suppose East takes ♡ 9
with ♡ 10, the outstanding ♡ Q is bound to fall next round. If, on the
other hand, West held four hearts ♡ 9 would win and three tricks
guaranteed. Now suppose that the finesse of ♠J had lost to ♠Q. South
must try for all four heart tricks. He must lead ♡ 4 from the table and
finesse ♡ J hoping for Q x or Q x x on his right. To play ♡ A first
would be a mistake as it could only hope to gain if ♡ Q were single. But
if ♡ Q were single with East, West would make a trick with ♡ 10 x x x.
And if ♡'Q were single with West, East with ♡ 10 8 7 3 would still
make a trick. On the other hand if East played ♡ Q on the initial lead
of ♡ 4 from dummy, South would be able to finesse against West's
♡ 10 with ♡ A 9 on the table.

Declarer's problem may not always be whether or not to make a
safety play. His tactics may also be affected by other factors such as:

    (a)   What alternative contract may be reached elsewhere.

    (b)   How well or badly he is doing.

    (c)   Whether a sacrifice bid may prove to be a 'phantom' and the
            adverse contract would not have succeeded.

Declarer's failure on this hand from a club duplicate event was
mainly careless but he had added reason for guarding against a bad
break.

South Dealer
Game All

North
♠ -
♡ K 10 8 6 4 2
◇ 7 4 3
♣ K 9 8 3

West
♠ J 10 9 8 6
♡ J 5
◇ A K Q 5 2
♣ 10

East
♠ 3
♡ A Q 7 3
◇ J 10 9 8 6
♣ 6 5 2

South
♠ A K Q 7 5 4 2
♡ 9
◇ -
♣ A Q J 7 4

After an Acol opening bid of two spades, South rebid clubs and proceeded to six clubs, after receiving heavy support.

West led ◊A which was ruffed and South drew trumps in three rounds. When the spades failed to break the hand got out of control and the contract was defeated by three tricks. South's excuse was that he was trying to make all thirteen tricks, which would only be possible if the spades divided evenly so that all dummy's hearts could be discarded and ♡9 ruffed. In this event any player bidding six spades would be successful and gain a bigger score, so that there was every reason to cater for a bad spade distribution, and ruff twice in dummy.

The effect of match point scoring is shewn in this hand from the World Pairs in Amsterdam.

East Dealer
East — West Vul.

```
                          North
                          ♠ A Q 3
                          ♡ Q 6 3
                          ◊ Q J 8
                          ♣ A 10 3 2
        West                                    East
        ♠ 10 9 8 5 4                            ♠ K 6
        ♡ K J 9                                 ♡ 4
        ◊ 6 5                                   ◊ A 10 9 4 3
        ♣ J 7 6                                 ♣ Q 9 8 5 4
                          South
                          ♠ J 7 2
                          ♡ A 10 8 7 5 2
                          ◊ K 7 2
                          ♣ K
```

with Lebiroda and Simon of Poland sitting North — South against Feldesman and Rubin, U.S.A, who finished eighth, the bidding was

S	W	N	E
2 H	-	2 NT	-
3 C	-	4 H	

South opened with a weak two bid and North's response was forcing, asking partner to describe his hand. The rebid of three clubs indicated the short suit. With this weakness pinpointed for the defence North decided to bid four hearts rather than three no trumps.

West led ♠10, dummy played low and ♠K won. East knew that South was short in clubs, so that he was likely to hold a few diamonds, leaving few for West. In order to preserve an entry he led a low diamond at trick two. This was taken with ◊Q and ♡3 was led to ♡A, and ♡2 returned. West went up with ♡K and returned his lone diamond and a ruff defeated the contract.

South was anxious to score better than those who might play in no trumps. Had it not been match pointed pairs he could have played safe by taking the first trick with ♠A and played trumps at once before the defence had time to organize a diamond ruff.

Belgians C. Monk and R. Silberwassen reached three no trumps against the eventual winners, C. Slavenberg and J. Kreyns from Holland, and made an extra overtrick when the Dutch East, in with ◊A, tried a desperation lead of ♠K.

If you are not doing well enough, in your assessment, it may be necessary to play "against the room", that is to say to adopt a line that is unlikely to be followed by other declarers, in the hope that it brings in some points. Desperation tactics seldom produce continued success but Rixi Markus gained a top in Amsterdam by deliberately playing against the odds.

East Dealer
Love All

```
                        North
                        ♠ A 10
                        ♡ J 6 3
                        ◊ A Q 9 8 7 2
                        ♣ J 2
        West                            East
        ♠ 8 6 2                         ♠ 9 4
        ♡ Q 7 5 4                       ♡ A K 10 9 8 2
        ◊ 6 5 4                         ◊ K
        ♣ K 8 3                         ♣ Q 10 5 4
                        South
                        ♠ K Q J 7 5 3
                        ♡ -
                        ◊ J 10 3
                        ♣ A 9 7 6
```

With Miss D. Shanahan and Mrs R. Markus (Great Britain) North — South opposing Mrs M. McGill and Mrs P. Smolinsky from Canada the bidding was

S	W	N	E
			1 H
2 S	-	3 D	-
4 S			

West led ♡4 ruffed in hand and at trick two Rixi Markus made the good psychological play of ◊J. It is too early in the hand for West to know what is going on and she might have covered. When West played low, ◊A was played from dummy and ◊K fell.

At the time this hand came up the British pair were a long way behind the leaders and points were badly needed. The percentage play is undoubtedly to finesse, but Mrs Markus had to play against the odds to gain on the board. As it was she made all thirteen tricks for a top which helped the British pair to finish fourth in the final order.

If you have made a sacrifice bid the play may be influenced by whether or not the opponents would have succeeded in their contract. This example from a Congress pairs illustrates the point.

West Dealer
East — West Vul.

```
                      North
                      ♠ 10 9 4 3
                      ♡ 5 2
                      ◊ A 7 3
                      ♣ A 8 5 2
West                                      East
♠ 5                                       ♠ Q 8 2
♡ A K Q 7 6                               ♡ J 9 8 3
◊ K Q J 9                                 ◊ 10 8 6
♣ J 10 7                                  ♣ K Q 9
                      South
                      ♠ A K J 7 6
                      ♡ 10 4
                      ◊ 5 4 2
                      ♣ 6 4 3
```

S	W	N	E
	1 H	-	2 H
2 S	4 H	4 S	-
-	Dbl.	-	-

South, at favourable vulnerability, intervened with two spades, mainly to indicate a lead in the event of West, as appeared likely, becoming declarer. North had a difficult problem over four hearts. With two aces there might be a chance of defeating the game but he decided that the defence would be unlikely to win many tricks in spades, especially if his partner held a six card suit, as well he might.

West cashed ♡ A and K and switched to ◇K, taken with ◇A. After one round of trumps won with ♠A, South crossed to dummy with ♣A and led ♠10, and had to decide whether to finesse or play for the drop. The normal play with a combined holding of nine cards, missing the queen, is to play out ace and king and hope the queen falls, but in this case the position was different. South realized that if he went four down by misguessing the trump he would lose 700, an almost certain bottom. Even if he lost only 500 it would be a disaster if four hearts was going down. South could see three defensive tricks with aces and if the spades were 2-2 it would mean that West would have four certain losers. Therefore South finessed ♠J on the second round on the assumption that the trumps were 3-1. He went only three down (500) which proved to be a good result as the majority of East – West pairs had scored 620 for making four hearts.

In judging whether a sacrifice bid is going to be a phantom, the essential factor if whether the opposing contract is likely to succeed, not whether it is theoretically possible to make. For example:

East Dealer
East — West Vul.

```
                    North
                    ♠ 7 4 2
                    ♡ A 8 2
                    ◇ 7 6 5 3
                    ♣ A 8 5
West                                        East
♠ Q 8 5 3                                   ♠ A J 10 9 6
♡ Q J 9 7                                   ♡ K 6
◇ A 9 8 4                                   ◇ Q J 10
♣ 10                                        ♣ Q 4 3
                    South
                    ♠ K
                    ♡ 10 5 4 3
                    ◇ K 2
                    ♣ K J 9 7 6 2
```

S	W	N	E
			1 S
2 C	3 S	4 C	4 S
5 C	-	-	Dbl.

West passed five clubs round to East who doubled, being uncertain of making five spades.

West led ♠3 to ♠A and ◇Q was returned. South ruffed the third round of diamonds and led a low club to dummy's ace and returned ♣5, East playing ♣4. Again, the problem was whether or not to finesse. The mere fact that East had doubled would not imply that he had the queen. South's bid was clearly sacrificial and East's double was obviously based on the expectations of defeating the contract on general strength. West's ♣10 might suggest that ♣Q was with it. The essential point was whether the other side would have made four spades. South could see one trick in hearts, one in clubs and a probable trick in spades. If clubs were 2-2 the game in spades was likely to fail. South finessed ♣J and lost only five tricks, the penalty of 500 proving above average, as most East — West pairs were forward bidders.

Of course there was no certainty that every East — West pair would reach four spades with a combined high card point total of 22. North — South were bound to fare badly against those who did not have game bid against them but the sacrifice would prove worth while if those who were in game made it. It will be noted that it was assumed that ♠K would make although it was unprotected. Once the ace is located on the right and it is apparent that the opponents have not such a large number of spades between them that they are likely to play for the drop, the bare king is likely to take a trick.

Sacrifice bids sometimes turn out far more successful than antici-pated. This hand from the Middlesex County Pairs Championship is an example.

East Dealer
East — West Vul.

North
♠ 6 5
♡ 6 4 3
◊ K 9 7
♣ A Q 10 9 5

West
♠ A Q 8 7 3
♡ Q 7
◊ Q 6 2
♣ K 7 4

East
♠ K J 4 2
♡ A J 10 9 8 5
◊ 4
♣ 8 3

South
♠ 10 9
♡ K 2
◊ A J 10 8 5 3
♣ J 6 2

S	W	N	E
			1 H
2 D	2 S	3 D	3 S
-	4 S	-	-
5 D	Dbl.		

West led ♠A and switched to ♡Q. East won with ♡A and returned ♡J to South's ♡K. Had he first cashed ♠K the contract would be down immediately but he may have formed the view that declarer had a singleton spade and that his partner would ruff the second heart. Be that as it may, South, being reprieved, took stock of the position. Against four spades South could see at least three tricks, with one diamond, one heart and one club. If diamonds were 2-2 there would be four top losers for the defence against four spades so that any minus score in five diamonds would be bad. Moreover if ♣K were with West four spades would be two down, with diamonds 2-2.

To avoid a bad board South needed to make his contract. As East had bid hearts and supported spades, he was more likely to be short in diamonds. Therefore if trumps were 3-1 it was more likely that East was short. It had also to be assumed that West held ♣K for five diamonds to be makeable.

After winning with ♡K, South led ◊A and successfully finessed against ◊Q. He drew the last trump with ◊K and returned to hand with a heart ruff and led ♣J. When the finesse succeeded he was able to discard his losing spade and make the doubled contract.

Tactics in Defence

Many match points are lost through failing to cash tricks while the opportunity remains. This is one of the problems created by match point conditions. You cannot afford to gamble if the overtrick that may be conceded may result in a zero score. Consider this situation:

```
              ♠ A 5
              ♡ A 6 5 4
              ◊ K Q 10 9
              ♣ 6 3 2
                         ♠ J 10 9 4
                         ♡ K J
                         ◊ A 3
                         ♣ A K Q J 9
```

With North — South vulnerable, East opened one club and raised West's response of one spade to four spades. North might have competed with a double over one spade, holding values in the unbid suits, but may have been deterred by the vulnerability.

North led ◊K, taken by ◊A, and ♠J was played and won by North's ♠A. After cashing ◊Q North was tempted to lead a low heart and give declarer a guess. If South held ♡Q the contract would very likely go down, for North having shewn up with ♠A and ◊K Q might well have taken action over one spade if he also held ♡A. But the risks are great. West may hold ♡Q himself or may guess right and play ♡K and later discard all his losers on the clubs. So it may be best to cash ♡A and keep declarer to his contract.

When the opposing bidding is strong it may be important to cash tricks quickly:

South Dealer
Game All

                          North
                          ♠ K 5 3
                          ♡ K 7
                          ◇ 4 3
                          ♣ A K Q J 9 8

West   East
♠ Q 8 6 4 2   ♠ 10 7
♡ 9 6 3   ♡ 10 5 4 2
◇ A K 2   ◇ 9 8 7 6 5
♣ 10 7   ♣ 6 3

                          South
                          ♠ A J 9
                          ♡ A Q J 8
                          ◇ Q J 10
                          ♣ 5 4 2

S	W	N	E
1 H	-	3 C	-
3 NT	-	-	-

When the hand was played in a club tournament many West players started off with ♠4, the fourth best of the longest suit. But on the strong North – South bidding there is very little chance of finding partner with any high cards, so there can be little point in trying to establish the spades. It is more important to save overtricks. Those who led ♠4 allowed declarer to make all thirteen tricks, with 3 spades, 4 hearts and 6 clubs. Those who cashed ♠A K and settled for eleven tricks did well.

One of the most difficult situations at match pointed pairs is to decide at what stage you abandon hope of defeating the enemy's contract and concentrate on saving overtricks. It is foreign to the nature of most players to give up the ghost and declarer is frequently presented with overtricks in a vain attempt to defeat the contract. In teams or rubber bridge it probably does not hurt to take a gamble to break a game or slam but which may give one or two extra tricks if it does not come off. But in match pointed pairs you cannot afford these attempts. If there is a long solid suit in dummy, which will provide discards for losers, it is better to cash. In other cases if there is a reasonable chance of defeating the contract if partner holds certain cards which will still be consistent with the bidding, then it is justifiable to try and set the contract.

A similar problem arises with the opening lead against a slam. Against a suit slam it is usually best to make an attacking lead in the hope of setting up a trick in case your side can get in early, possibly through a losing finesse, or a high card that declarer needs to force out. This means that certain risks may have to be taken by leading from a king or queen, which may give an overtrick. In team events this will not matter but it may in pairs.

Here again it is difficult to lay down rules, but in the main it is advisable to take the risk if there is, in your opinion, the remotest chance of beating the slam. It is quite likely that the slam will not always be called so you will get a poor result anyway and the overtrick will not matter so much. If the bidding has been confident you are better to lead out an ace. If the slam is a lay down you may salvage something by taking one trick when an alternative lead may allow all thirteen tricks to be made.

In attempting to appraise the contract the following very general rules may serve as a rough guide.

1. If you are in a part score with a minority of the points you have probably done well to buy the contract. If any penalty is kept below 150 the result should be reasonable as a part score is likely to be made by the other side. However, do not risk the loss of 150 or more in an effort to make the contract.

2. If you are doubled in one no trump with a combined total of 16 points and the opponents are vulnerable, try to keep the penalty down to 500. The opponents may well have game, in which case your loss will compare favourably with the 600 or so they might have scored. Of course, if they cannot make game, or it is not reasonably biddable, you are likely to do badly even if you get out for a loss of 300. Your only chance is that game will be bid and made at other tables, in which case you must concentrate on not losing more than 500.

   If your combined count is 17 or more, an adverse game is unlikely and you must try and go no more than one trick down, losing 100. If you are vulnerable the loss of 200 is probably fatal, so you must take risks to try and make the contract.

3. If you are in a no trump contract the following scale is an approximate guide as to the number of tricks you should hope to make. In each case it is assumed that there is no long suit.

19-20-21	7 tricks	Some will go down or the hand may be thrown in.
22-23	8 tricks	Making two no trumps on 22 will probably be good.
24	8 tricks	If you are in two no trumps and the hand goes well you may get 9-10 tricks. In this case there is the danger that some will be in game, particularly if each hand contains 12 points, where the bidding may be one no trump – three no trumps. If you have reached game you can afford to make a safety play to ensure the contract, as others may well be in a part score.
25-26	9 tricks	Most are likely to bid game, but such contracts are not always lay down. You can afford to make certain.
27-29	10 tricks	
30-31	10-11 tricks	If twelve tricks are certain there is a risk of someone bidding and making a slam. You should hope to make eleven tricks after losing a finesse or a suit breaking badly.

If the contract you have reached is altogether out of this world there is nothing you can do but try and make it, whatever the cost. As no-one else is likely to have thought of it, you must hope for miracles; otherwise it is certain to be a bottom.

Estimation of Match Points

Most players like to estimate the number of match points they expect to receive on each board, so as to have a rough idea as to whether they are doing well or badly. It is also useful when comparing with the actual figures after the result of the contest. In this way a mistake in the match pointing may be spotted.

Take a simple example. You have been given one point on a board for which you reckoned you would get a top. It will be wise to ask to inspect the travelling score slip and check up. It is only too easy for a mistake to be made, especially as most Tournament Directors try to get results out with the minimum of delay.

Although with experience it is possible to achieve quite a high standard of accuracy in the estimation of match points, any such assessment can, at best, be an approximate guide only. This at least enables you to see whether you are above or below average by a top or half a top. There are some who will state after a session that their score is 59½%, or that they are three tops over average. To be too definite is foolish, for it frequently turns out that one's estimate proves to be erroneous and such boastful claims end up in disappointment and quite often in ridicule.

Some pairs tournaments are large and run in sections, all playing the same boards which have been duplicated. Sometimes the tournament is held in several different towns, as in the case of the British Bridge League Portland Club Cup for mixed pairs.

The British Bridge League and English Bridge Union hold simultaneous pairs tournaments where pre-duplicated boards are played on the same night in clubs in all parts of the world. The results are all sent in to London and match pointed over all, the top being astronomical.

Clearly it is quite impossible to make an accurate forecast of your score when you never see the results in other sections or in other venues. In big tournaments it is better to use a simple method of estimating such as:

> Average
> Average plus
> Average minus

You can, if you like, add "good" or "bad" for results which are near tops and bottoms. An unexpected penalty of 1400 would qualify in this category as also would an oppenent's grand slam call missing the ace of trumps. There surely will not be many others making the same error!

The following suggestions may prove helpful in estimating match points:

1. Adopt a cautious outlook on early boards. With no other scores to guide you it is difficult to forecast what will happen. Do not claim a top or bottom unless some spectacular result has occurred that is unlikely to be repeated. For example, a penalty of 800 or 1100 when neither side could make more than a part score, or

you have been doubled into game when there was no apparent reason.

You are fairly safe to expect a better than average score if:

(a) You have collected a penalty of 150 or more when only a part score was available for your side.

(b) You have stopped in three hearts or three spades when only nine tricks were possible. You can afford to be more optimistic if game depends on a finesse which is wrong.

(c) The opponents play in game in a minor suit holding stoppers in all four suits. If they make eleven tricks it is certain they could have done better in no trumps.

2. As stated earlier, you are probably due for a good result if you play the contract with a minority of the points and either make it or lose 100 or less. But sometimes caution is needed. If you buy the contract in two spades, going down by two tricks, not vulnerable (-100) and you and your partner hold only 15 points between you, it is tempting to assume that you have a wonderful result. The danger is that opponents may reach three no trumps and go down and your minus score will not compare with others in your line who have registered a plus.

3. Be careful not to over-estimate if opponents are vulnerable. Suppose you play in two hearts and make ten tricks owing to very poor defence, you are inclined to claim a top. But if opponents are vulnerable and have enough to enter the bidding they may lose 200.

4. Should the enemy bid and make a game that is quite unbeatable, do not necessarily expect an average unless it is apparent that game is easy to reach. For example:

<pre>
          ♠ Q 6 5 2
          ♡ K 7 4 3
          ◊ A 7 6 5
          ♣ 8

          ♠ A K J 8 2
          ♡ 8 3
          ◊ 4 3 2
          ♣ A 7 6
</pre>

South opened one spade and North bid four spades. Trumps were 2-2 and the ace of hearts was with West, under the king, so the contract could not be defeated. But it was bound to be a bad result for East — West, for South had a minimum opener and North stretched his hand to bid four spades. Certainly more would be out of game than in it. Here is a further example from a club tournament.

North Dealer
North — South Vul.

```
                        North
                        ♠ K Q J 8 6 4
                        ♡ K 10
                        ◇ J 4 2
                        ♣ A 2
    West                                    East
    ♠ 5 3                                   ♠ A 2
    ♡ J 5                                   ♡ A 9 8 6
    ◇ K Q 10 7 3                            ◇ A 5
    ♣ K Q 10 3                              ♣ 9 8 7 6 4
                        South
                        ♠ 10 9 7
                        ♡ Q 7 4 3 2
                        ◇ 9 8 6
                        ♣ J 5
```

S	W	N	E
		1 S	-
-	2 D	-	2 H
-	3 C	-	5 C

East's bid of two hearts was a little unorthodox but it served its purpose and gave his partner the chance to bid clubs.

North led ♠K and dummy's second spade was discarded on the third diamond. Declarer lost one club and one heart, scoring 400. Here again, despite the fact that game was undefeatable, North — South must get a bad result as five clubs is not easy to reach. It is also lucky as the diamonds have to split 3-3 to enable a losing spade to be discarded before drawing trumps.

At two tables North was allowed to play in one spade which he made.

It is almost always over-optimistic to assume an average if a slam is bid and made against you. Apart from those occasions where the hands are so overwhelmingly strong, it is rare for a slam to be bid by every partnership.

5. Your assessment of match points may be affected by the play of the hand. If declarer has felled your queen by playing for the drop when the better percentage was to finesse, you are likely, through no fault of your own, to get a poor score. Or if you are opposed by an expert who makes an overtrick by a squeeze, or brings home a difficult contract, you are likely to come off worse than others.

If you have played normally, but the result has been disastrous you are not necessarily booked for a bottom. What has happened to you can happen to others.

It is easy to over-estimate your score in a situation such as this:

        ♠ K 4
        ♡ 10 6
        ◊ A Q J 8 5 2
        ♣ Q 8 5

        ♠ A 7 2
        ♡ Q J 2
        ◊ K 4
        ♣ A K 10 9 3

You are South in three no trumps. West leads ♣ Q and you take all thirteen tricks and expect to get a top as the opponents could have cashed the ♡ A and ♡ K. If West's hand turns out to be something like this

    ♠ Q J 10 9 3   ♡ K 5 4 3   ◊ 10 3   ♣ J 2

the result is almost certain to be universal as everyone with the hand is going to lead ♣ Q. The only feature that might alter the position is if North were to play the hand, giving East the lead. But with the weakness in hearts, South is more likely to bid no trumps first. The probable sequence will be either

S	N	S	N
1 C	1 D	1 NT	3 NT
2 NT	3 NT		

More difficult to assess are those evenly distributed hands played in three no trumps, where nine tricks are virtually certain if North is declarer and defeat is likely if South plays the hand. So much depends on the bidding and the system employed as to which partner first bids no trumps.

6. Take the personal factor into consideration and notice the calibre of the players in your line. Assume that in a Mitchell movement you are at table four, an inexperienced pair are at table five and a strong pair at table three. The boards move down each round so that you receive yours from the weak pair at table five and your results are liable to be flattering and you may be induced to think that your result is better than it really is. When the boards move on the strong pair may well do better and devalue your result.

A certain well known London player is apt to become quite depressed if her result is inferior to that of the pair who have just played the board. Her immediate reaction is that it must be a bottom. In such a case as this it is wise to ensure that you do not sit at the table from which you will receive boards from a strong pair as their good results may cause momentary depression and gloom.

Again, if a slam is bid and made against you, look to see which other pairs in their line are also likely to reach it.

Individual Tournaments

There is very little advice that can be given for this type of competition. The element of luck is very great and likely to influence the result far more than any preconceived tactical plan.

Since you have to play with every other competitor, each being an unfamiliar partner, it is best to play a safe straightforward game, avoiding bids that might be misconstrued.

As only one board might be played with each partner there is no point in entering into a lengthy discussion on systems and conventions. It makes the event long drawn out and slow. A good method is that adopted by the English Bridge Union at their Summer Congress in Brighton and probably used by other organizing bodies elsewhere.

A natural basic system is laid down (e.g. Acol) and certain basic conventions stipulated. For example

> No Trumps 12-14   15-17
>   Lower Minor over Pre-emptive Opening Bids
> Stayman.   Unusual No Trump.   Blackwood.

This type of thing serves to cut down unnecessary discussion between partners who are only due to play one, or perhaps two, boards together. You are also likely to do well if you put your partner at his or her ease. With careful handling even the weakest player is capable of rising to the occasion. This advice, of course, should apply to all forms of bridge, both duplicate and rubber. Apart from increasing your chance of success, it will certainly add to the enjoyment.

9

ILLUSTRATIVE HANDS

TEAMS · IMP SCORING

Safety Play

With IMP scoring a safety play that ensures the contract is recommended, even though it may concede a trick. An overtrick is of little value compared with the value of game.

This hand is from the Teams Championship at the English Bridge Union Congress at Eastbourne, 1958.

South Dealer
East — West Vul.

North
♠ A K 5 4
♡ A J
♦ J 7 3
♣ 6 5 3 2

West
♠ J 9 8 7
♡ 10 8 6 4 3 2
♦ K 9 5
♣ -

East
♠ Q 3
♡ K 9
♦ Q 8 6 4 2
♣ Q 10 9 7

South
♠ 10 6 2
♡ Q 7 5
♦ A 10
♣ A K J 8 4

S	W	N	E
1 C	-	1 S	-
1 NT	-	3 NT	-

West led ♡ 4 and North played dummy's ♡ A. It would be risky to finesse in case East wins and returned a diamond. South next led ♣ 2 and covered East's ♣ 7 with ♣ 8. Had West won, the remaining clubs would have fallen to ♣A and ♣ K, giving declarer 4 clubs, 2 spades 1 diamond and 1 heart. The ninth trick would come from hearts, unless West switched to a diamond, in which case a second trick would be made in the suit.

If South plays ♣J on the first club lead he cannot avoid East making a club trick and a diamond lead from the right will allow the defence to make five tricks before declarer can make nine.

PAIRS · MATCH POINTS

Safety Play in Slam Contract

A safety play to ensure a slam contract is advisable even in match pointed pairs events as an above average score is probable. This hand occurred in a club duplicate tournament.

South Dealer
Love All

                      North
                      ♠ A K 4
                      ♡ K 3
                      ◇ 3 2
                      ♣ A Q 9 7 6 4

West   East
♠ 9 6 5   ♠ 7 3
♡ J 9 5   ♡ A 8 6 2
◇ Q J 10   ◇ 9 8 7 6 5 4
♣ J 8 5 3   ♣ 2

                      South
                      ♠ Q J 10 8 2
                      ♡ Q 10 7 4
                      ◇ A K
                      ♣ K 10

South is declarer in six spades and West leads ◇Q.

South leads ♠Q followed by ♠2 to ♠A. When both opponents follow suit he plays ♣4 to ♣K and ♣10 to ♣Q. If clubs are 3-2 he merely draws the last trump and runs the clubs to make all thirteen tricks. The play has provided for the existing distribution where the clubs are 4-1 and the hand with the singleton has only two trumps and cannot ruff. A low club is ruffed in hand and dummy entered with ♠K and the clubs cashed.

If the trumps had proved to be 4-1 there would be no alternative but to play off ♠K, enter the closed hand with ♣K and draw the remaining trump, hoping the clubs will split 3-2.

South's actual play was correct for an additional reason. Some pairs might be in six no trumps which would gain a better score if it made, as it would if the clubs were evently distributed. There was, therefore, added reason to cater for a 4-1 club break which would defeat the no trump addicts.

TEAMS. AGGREGATE SCORING

The principle of "if in doubt bid one more" is illustrated on this hand from the Hubert Phillips Bowl, Mixed Teams Championship of the English Bridge Union.

West Dealer
North — South Vul.

```
                    North
                    ♠ K Q J 7 6 3
                    ♡ A 2
                    ◇ -
                    ♣ A K J 7 6
West                                      East
♠ A 10 2                                  ♠ -
♡ Q 9 8 4                                 ♡ K J 7 6 5 3
◇ Q J 10 6 3 2                            ◇ A 9 8 7 5 4
♣ -                                       ♣ Q
                    South
                    ♠ 9 8 5 4
                    ♡ 10
                    ◇ K
                    ♣ 10 9 8 5 4 3 2
```

In Room One the bidding was

S	W	N	E
	1 D	2 D	5 D
-	-	5 S	6 D
6 S	Dbl.		

East led ◊ A and the contract was made for a score of 1660. A club lead would have defeated the contract but East had no good reason to lead ♣ Q. If he interprets West's double as Lightner, asking for an "unusual lead" he would be more likely to try a heart, hoping for a void in partner's hand.

In Room Two the bidding was

S	W	N	E
	1 D	2 D	6 D
Dbl.			

It is not quite clear why South doubled. North led ♣ A and the contract was made for a further gain of 1090. The slam would be defeated by the lead of ♡ A and ♡ 2 but even if North starts off with ♡ A he is likely to try and cash ♣ A at trick 2 as he has no reason to place South with all the rest of the clubs and West with none.

TEAMS. AGGREGATE SCORING

Safety Play

In a pre-war match between Austria and Hungary the same safety play was made by both declarers to ensure a slam contract.

South Dealer

Game All

```
                        North
                        ♠ J 4 3 2
                        ♡ Q 5
                        ◇ 2
                        ♣ K 10 7 6 5 4
West                                        East
♠ K Q 10 9 5                                ♠ 8 7 6
♡ -                                         ♡ 8 7 4 3 2
◇ 10 9 8 6 5 3                              ◇ -
♣ J 3                                       ♣ A Q 9 8 2
                        South
                        ♠ A
                        ♡ A K J 10 9 6
                        ◇ A K Q J 7 4
                        ♣ -
```

South was declarer in six hearts, doubled by East. West led ♠K won with ♠A.

To ensure the contract South led a low diamond at trick 2. It was now possible to ruff ◇7 with ♡Q and make the rest.

If South were to draw trumps he would lose two diamonds. If he led ◇A earlier, East could ruff and return a trump.

Temptation to Play in a Major rather than a Minor Suit

A slam bid and made is seldom a bad result and it is more important to ensure that you are in the safest contract than to worry too much whether it is a major or minor suit. Several pairs neglected this principle to their cost in the World Mixed Pairs in Amsterdam.

West Dealer
Game All

	North	
	♠ K 6 5	
	♡ 10 6	
	◊ K Q J 7 4	
	♣ 7 6 4	

West		East
♠ Q J 7		♠ A 8 4 2
♡ 8 7 2		♡ 9 5
◊ 9 5 3		◊ 10 6
♣ Q 8 5 3		♣ K J 10 9 2

	South	
	♠ 10 9 3	
	♡ A K Q J 4 3	
	◊ A 8 2	
	♣ A	

South opened fourth in hand with two hearts (Acol) and received a response of three diamonds. Hoping for a higher score South finished in six hearts and was defeated by the lead of ♠Q. No lead could defeat six diamonds. 6NT played by North is also safe.

PAIRS. MATCH POINTS

Value of Overtricks

This hand from the World Mixed Pairs in Amsterdam illustrates the value of overtricks in match pointed pairs.

North Dealer
North – South Vul.

	North
	♠ A J 5
	♡ Q J 10 4
	◇ A J 3
	♣ K Q 9

West	East
♠ 4 2	♠ 10 9
♡ A 5 2	♡ 9 8 7
◇ K 8 6 5 4	◇ Q 10 9 7
♣ 8 7 5	♣ A J 6 4

	South
	♠ K Q 8 7 6 3
	♡ K 6 3
	◇ 2
	♣ 10 3 2

S	W	N	E
		1 H	-
1 S	-	2 NT	-
4 S	-	-	-

When West led a club and an honour was played from dummy, only five East players ducked and allowed the honour to hold. When West later gained the lead with ♡ A and continued clubs, East made ♣ A J to hold the contract to ten tricks. Making an overtrick was worth 75 out of 128 match points for North – South. Making no overtrick gave North – South only 10 points, a net difference of 65 match points on the first trick.

Safety Play

Declarer's safety play was rewarded in a spectacular fashion in this hand from a team of four match.

South Dealer
Love All

```
                      North
                      ♠ Q
                      ♡ A J 8
                      ◊ Q J 8
                      ♣ A Q J 9 4 3
West                                      East
♠ J 9 3 2                                 ♠ K 8 7 5 4
♡ 7 3                                     ♡ K 10 9 6
◊ 10 9 2                                  ◊ 7 6 4
♣ 10 8 7 2                                ♣ K
                      South
                      ♠ A 10 6
                      ♡ Q 5 4 2
                      ◊ A K 5 3
                      ♣ 6 5
```

South opened one no trump (12-14) and was raised to three no trumps. West led ♠2 covered by ♠Q, ♠K and ♠A. South next led ♣6 and played ♣A, felling East's ♣K. South's play was designed to prevent East getting in to return a spade and catered for the one situation where East might get the lead when it could have been avoided, namely with a singleton ♣K. If West held ♣K it would not matter and if East held it guarded nothing could be done.

PAIRS. MATCH POINTS

Safety Play in Slam Contract

A safety play that conceded a trump trick in spite of holding a seven card suit headed by all five honours proved a good investment on this hand from a Charity Congress in Richmond, England.

South Dealer
North — South Vul.

```
                    North
                    ♠ 8 6 5 4
                    ♡ A K Q 4
                    ◇ 8 7
                    ♣ 8 6 4
West                                    East
♠ 10 2                                  ♠ K J 9 7
♡ 6 5 3                                 ♡ J 10 9 8 7 2
◇ 9 4 3                                 ◇ 2
♣ Q J 10 9 7                            ♣ 5 2
                    South
                    ♠ A Q 3
                    ♡ -
                    ◇ A K Q J 10 6 5
                    ♣ A K 3
```

This proved to be a most frustrating hand and most South players went down in grand slams, being unable to reach dummy's hearts. One lucky declarer in seven diamonds received the lead of ◇3 from West who had been told to lead a trump against a grand slam. This put the lead in dummy and ♡ A K Q looked after ♠Q 3 and ♣3.

Those in six diamonds or six no trumps by South did well if they led a low diamond to the table. This sacrificed a trick in diamonds but made certain of reaching the hearts with either ◇8 or ◇7.

PAIRS. MATCH POINTS

Safety Play　　　　　　*Safety Play*

A play that gives declarer an additional chance is correct playing match pointed pairs, as shewn in this hand from a club tournament.

South Dealer
East — West Vul.

```
                  North
                  ♠ 6 3 2
                  ♡ A 8 5 4
                  ◊ J 5
                  ♣ 7 5 4 3
West                              East
♠ 9 7                            ♠ 10 8 5
♡ Q 10 2                         ♡ K J 9 3
◊ Q 10 8 4 2                     ◊ 9 3
♣ K Q J                          ♣ 10 9 8 2
                  South
                  ♠ A K Q J 4
                  ♡ 7 6
                  ◊ A K 7 6
                  ♣ A 6
```

S	W	N	E
2 S	-	2 NT	-
3 D	-	4 S	-

West leads ♣K, taken with ♣A. It is tempting to play ◊A K and ruff a diamond, but this fails when East is able to over-ruff.

South can increase his chances by leading a low diamond at trick 2. If West has ◊Q, as here, he has three diamond tricks. If East holds ◊Q, South has not given up the chance of ruffing the third round of diamonds on the table.

It Can Only be a Bottom

On this hand from a club pairs tournament in London, declarer in three no trumps doubled and redoubled failed to take a trick and lost 3400.

South Dealer
East — West Vul.

```
                          North
                          ♠ J 9 2
                          ♡ Q 8 5
                          ◇ A K 9 2
                          ♣ K 8 6
       West                                      East
       ♠ A 6                                     ♠ Q 10 8 7 5 4
       ♡ A K 6 2                                 ♡ 9 7 3
       ◇ J 3                                     ◇ 5
       ♣ 9 7 5 4 3                               ♣ A Q J
                          South
                          ♠ K 3
                          ♡ J 10 4
                          ◇ Q 10 8 7 6 4
                          ♣ 10 2
```

S	W	N	E
-	-	1 D	1 S
1 NT	3 S	-	-
3 NT	Dbl.	Redbl.	

West led ♡A and switched to a low club taken with ♣J. East returned a heart to ♡K and the club return captured dummy's ♣K. After cashing ♣Q, East returned a low spade. South could have earned a trick in spades by playing low, but going four down redoubled would be a zero, so he gambled by playing ♠K. Had this held he could take six diamonds and be two down losing 600. This might be worth a few points if East — West could make a vulnerable game. But West captured ♠K with ♠A, played off his two good clubs and led back a spade for East to win the rest of the tricks. 3 NT** − 9 = − 3400 is an unusual entry.

TEAMS. IMP SCORING

This hand from the Welsh Bridge Union Congress in Porthcawl is a further instance of declarer failing to take a trick.

South Dealer
East — West Vul.

North
♠ A Q J 4
♡ A J 7 6
◇ 10 5 2
♣ 8 3

West
♠ K 10 6 5
♡ Q 10 8 4 2
◇ -
♣ A K 6 5

East
♠ 9 8 7 3
♡ K 9
◇ K 4
♣ Q J 10 9 7

South
♠ 2
♡ 5 3
◇ A Q J 9 8 7 6 3
♣ 4 2

S	W	N	E
3 D	3 H	-	3 S
-	4 S	Dbl.	4 NT
-	-	Dbl.	-

West's bid of three hearts was Fishbein asking partner to take out into a suit. East bid the major suit in preference to the minor and West should have passed the forced bid. East hoped to make ◇K when he removed to four no trumps.

South led ♠2 and East tried to get in early by playing ♠K. North won and returned ◇10 and declarer was faced with having to find a great many discards. It is easy to slip up when confronted with disaster and East parted with too many spades so that North was able to win the last four tricks with ♠Q J 4 and ♡ A. North — South + 2900.

This was a hand from the qualifying round and the team that gained this penalty failed to qualify. Had it been aggregate scoring it would have been quite different.